Jyoti Barmola Mamgain is the multitalented wife of an officer in the Indian Army. With a wide array of interests spanning social work, event management, travel, baking, art, and writing, she effortlessly blends creativity with purpose. During her decade-long career as a professional event manager, she orchestrated prestigious events across India. Notably, she also oversaw the design and production of the bestselling coffee-table book, *The Indians*, which highlighted the interesting aspects and extraordinary facets of common people of the country. In her avatar as a fauji wife, she has managed the welfare of over 150 families, organized high-profile events, and skilfully balanced multiple responsibilities. She was honoured by the Army Wives Welfare Association (AWWA) in 2019 for her work. She lives life to the fullest while raising two children. She continues to create value through her contributions to society and her vibrant fauji life.

Praise for the Book

'This hilarious book will make us veterans laugh aloud as we relive our glorious years in the army.' – Lt Gen Rajinder Singh, PVSM, UYSM, SM (Retd) and Mrs Usha Singh

'Fifteen years have passed since we meticulously planned a memorable fauji welcome for Jyoti as a daughter of our fauji family. Jyoti's #ROFL narration of it in *Drills, Thrills and Spills* brought tears to our eyes – she has grown to herself grooming Gen Z daughters (and sons) into the fauj using traditions that make Fevicol bonds. She explains the army's organizational culture used to build and nurture relations necessary to meet our national security goals. Her tales about how officers in uniform and their spouses learn to turn adversities into adventures and limitations into opportunities make this a good read for both young and aspiring soldiers, and their spouses. Jyoti serves a gentle reminder that finding happiness in adversity is a matter of choice – for the fauji, the fauji's spouse and their children.' – Maj Gen Sanjay P. Vishwasrao, SM**, and Mrs Sanjeevani S. Vishwasrao

'Entertaining and refreshing, this book offers a precious and often hilarious glimpse behind the scenes of the life of the Indian Army wife. With true-life anecdotes and unique lived experiences, the author brings alive the highs and lows of being a fauji wife, from falling in love with an army man, to the tribulations of constant postings, the infinite challenges of setting up home in remote locations and much more. Written with a good dose of wry humour, self-awareness and sensitivity, this book is a must read for anyone who would like to know the reality of the lives of the women who are the backbones of the brave men who guard our nation. Salute to their grit and spirit!' – Kiran Manral, bestselling author

DRILLS, THRILLS AND SPILLS

AN ARMY WIFE'S TALES

JYOTI BARMOLA MAMGAIN

Om Books International

Reprinted in 2025

Om Books International

Corporate & Editorial Office
A-12, Sector 64, Noida 201 301
Uttar Pradesh, India
Phone: +91 120 477 4100
Email: editorial@ombooks.com
Website: www.ombooksinternational.com

Sales Office
107, Ansari Road, Darya Ganj,
New Delhi 110 002, India
Phone: +91 11 4000 9000
Email: sales@ombooks.com
Website: www.ombooks.com

Illustrations by Col S. Ramesh, SM

ISBN: 978-93-6395-680-3

Printed in India

10 9 8 7 6 5 4 3 2

To my parents Mr B.R. Barmola (late) and
Mrs Jayanti Barmola
I am what I am because of you.

Contents

Preface

Books! They work differently for different people. For some literary enthusiasts, they are like a daily dose of 'vitamin read' that nourishes their minds and souls. Their imagination soars with every page they read, and by merely sitting in one place, they float along with the story. Such readers feel the book, and for them, it's an essential part of their lives. These readers are often tagged as 'bookworms', experiencing the colours of life through those black-and-white pages.

For some, books work as an apparatus to ace the art of rhetoric, especially for those born as Gen X and Gen Y, who were raised in this epoch of high-tech times where everything is a click away. They place extra emphasis on enhancing their vocabulary through extensive reading. This lot of readers, who focus mainly on complicated and arduous King's English, approach their reading more practically.

Amusingly, for many people, books work as an accessory to flaunt. Books for them are bought and kept in shelves as decoration pieces and are often used only for bragging. 'Oh, you know, I have the whole set of Charles Dickens's work.' What they leave unsaid is: Well, they look so good on the shelf, I have never taken them out to read.

Whatever category we might belong to, many of us must have experienced the joy of roaming around in a fancy, air-conditioned bookshop (with designer coffee bars or tearooms as is the trend these days) in the posh markets of our metro cities. Or visiting booksellers on the streets of Janpath or Nai Sarak, with their bargain price 'cover' versions, and, if you have the eye, a rare find. Unless we are very clear of what book or author we want to buy, a random search might lead us to a catchy title; after all, the industry of designing dust jackets and cover art does make a substantial difference.

During such desultory explorations, words like 'yoga', 'weight-loss', 'positive thinking, 'aura', 'world peace', etc., ring a bell hard enough to evoke curiosity. In our country, one of the many such popular genres is 'Indian Army', 'Bharatiya Sena' or 'Fauj', which also catches the eye of a true Indian reader. I give credit for this partly to the patriotic genes present abundantly in every Indian and partly to the curiosity of every civilian about the army way of life, how it functions, what world lies beyond the cantonment walls, and, above all, the most general question every time we meet our civilian friends: '*Tumhari life badi serious aur disciplined hogi*?' (You must lead a serious and disciplined life?) The general inquisitiveness about the lives of army personnel is insane! Though books and films do provide some ideas about army life, as they say, '*Kahani abhi baaki hai*!'

We know that the Indian Army is a well-groomed organisation where almost everything, starting from recruiting soldiers to his training and grooming is done without any compromises. A soldier's hard work and devotion to duty is quite unparalleled, and I can say without a doubt that no other citizen is called upon to exercise his duty as much as a soldier is. Then there is the family. The sacrifices an army family, particularly a soldier's wife, is called upon to make can be daunting for the most hardened individual.

Being an army wife myself, I believe that through our husbands, the love for our nation seeps into us and our kids. We are ready for all adjustments and sacrifices we have to make as a family, always ready to support them in everything they do, and respect the decisions which, most of the time, are not made with family priorities in mind. We stand shoulder to shoulder with them to live by their motto of 'nation above all.'

However, unlike most books, documentaries, and interviews that celebrate the glory of army soldiers and their heroic deeds, I do not intend to show you our world from the same perspective. I want to talk about the flip side of life behind the crisp olive-green uniforms. As the Hindi film song goes, '*Parde ke peechhe kya hai*?' No. Rest assured. There is nothing salacious or scandalous. This is not a tell-all memoir.

However, the solemn demeanour and the starched uniforms do hide a thousand last-minute adjustments. The façade takes some effort to build and nurture. The adversities they face do make them live to the fullest – giving rise to the stereotypical image of the hail-fellow-well-met army man – but there's more to an army person's life than strict adherence to deadlines and schedules and ranks. Or let's say: the strict adherence makes for delightful behind-the-scenes stories.

So, whatever heroic stories you may have heard about the Indian Army with its larger-than-life image, let me unravel the common side, the simple things they experience – such as laughing heartily, eating thoughtlessly, buying groceries, watching movies, cartoon shows and daily soaps, and finally domestic squabbles with spouses, which are a common sight in our homes too.

Changing times and modernity have affected almost every aspect of life, including our culture, traditions, and rituals. However, unlike in the civilian world, where it has influenced many practices, the Indian Army chose to stick to the basics. It has never lost its belief in the richness of our culture, traditions, and heritage, and has carried along the legacy of military ethics passed from one generation of soldiers and their families to another. Not just the practice of discipline, punctuality, the dress code, but the culture, including the softer sides of life, like emotions, love, sympathy, and compassion. It has emphasised living a life with the utmost standards of human character. We believed in and created a way of life which was worth living and dying for.

I narrate here how, as a family and as an army wife, we have our own experiences and stories to tell. How hailing from a civilian background, we enter this mystical world strongly rooted in its cultures and traditions and how it changes our outlook on life. The book also aims to make its readers experience the never-seen-never-heard anecdotes of an Indian Army wife on the domestic battlefront. The 'encounters' she survives with style, grace, and laughter. The experiences that make life worthy of living every single day. It also reveals the softer side of our soldiers, equally domesticated (in its own way), hilarious, casual, experiential, and different from how we have viewed it as outsiders.

We laugh, we cry, we grow together, we celebrate our challenges, sacrifices, and sometimes austerities and yet make bonds that are worth a thousand lifetimes. With all the serious work involving the defence of the nation happening on one hand, the other hand has its own entertainment quotient, own actors, and own drama…

So, let the show begin!

1

Masala

While living a comfortable life in a metro city, not even in my dreams had I thought that someday I would be breathing in places where having a Wi-Fi connection would be a luxury. Now, after more than a decade of living as an army wife, I have realized that it was not just about Wi-Fi connections.

On occasional free Sundays, random thoughts of missing out on the happening things in life, especially after spending one or two dedicated, intense hours of Facebook- and Instagram-ing, often hits a fauji wife's mind like a tsunami. Seeing how your peers enjoy and experience the pleasures of urban existence often results in the usual, healthy domestic wrangles with oblivious military husbands (who are often without social media accounts). Such *fauji ghar ki ladai* (arguments in a military household), like most *aam ghar ki ladai* (arguments of the general household), across the country on Sundays, brings forth various popular reference: the topmost being the count of scarifies done by military wives to keep the marriage wheels rolling, fuelled by strong references to regular domestic complaints.

Given that the fauji wife functions as a supporting wheel to enable the true-blue military lifestyle, she has more arrows in her quiver to shoot at her guardless fauji husband at home. At such moments, references to feeding aloo parathas to course mates with ravenous appetites at any time of the day or night, attending parties in uncomfortable saris and heels, managing the social calendar for the whole year, and surviving on limited government salaries come to the fore. And last but not least, it eventually leads to the kids, the emotional trump card, the Brahmastra, of any Indian lady.

We shoot ruthlessly with throat-chocked, weepy allegations, the most common one among fauji wives being: 'The last time my kids entered a shopping mall, they believed it was Disney World! It's all because of you and your job! And the hinterlands we get posted to.'

The other, most popular, grievance of the newlywed fauji wives, at the peak of bristling with rage, usually start with: 'The last time we ate in a fancy restaurant, half of the month's salary just got swiped away! I left my job, city … Blah! blah! blah!' Such scenes are a normal sight in any military household. After all, the ever-optimist fauji believes, 'You have to fight through some bad days to earn the best days of your life.'

However, everything eventually gets sorted in life when you live with a man crafted to be chivalrous enough. Such 'fury' evenings often end with a simple chilled glass of wine bought at subsidized rates from the military canteens, and some classic music playing on YouTube, which work instantly and calm a fauji wife down without fail.

However, before you start believing too much in fairytales, I must say that even romantic evenings have a deadline in a military home. No matter how intense the romantic moment is or how grave the issue, a typical military husband has an invisible soldierly clock ticking in his mind all the time, and all the drama, whatever it may be, must end by 9 p.m. – or to put it in more military-sounding terms, by 2100 hours – because he needs to get up early in the morning for the eternal daily physical training (PT) routine. Thus in a military home, fights and romance, roothna and manana are also timed. One must literally shut down all the windows because the system of our hardwired husbands has to restart early in the morning.

So far, the story must be relatable to all the readers. After all, a fauji married life has a similar flavour to all other civilian marriages. However, what is different is the *tadka* on it. And that, in our case, is definitely Olive Green!

But wait! *Tadka se pehle, dal galni chahiye na*! (Before the tadka, the dal needs to be cooked, right!) So, let's talk about the courtship period.

2

Civilian Pyaar

Like a typical Indian girl brought up in a deshbhakt family, having a military beau is a matter of immense pride. But for a young Delhi damsel, it comes with a dash of swank. Who doesn't like to go for a coffee and flaunt 'the man' who dares to jump from jets, ride tanks, glide in parachutes, is as fit as Rambo, loves sports and is as chivalrous as a knight. One feels nothing less than dating a desi Mr Bond!

Before I go further, I want to shed some feminine light on the word 'flaunt' and how it works very differently with each woman, depending on her hormones. The way a woman flaunts (a thing, possession, or a person in my case) can vary from one to another. She may look casual in her approach, but beware, you ignorant souls! She is attentive and hyper-vigilant about each move. She knows the language of the eyes and, as she casually flaunts at her own pace, it sublimely empowers her mentally and emotionally. Her awareness of her asset elevates her mood, and the glow will tell you that she knows what she has, and it's worth a show.

I enjoyed every moment of it unapologetically!

However, at ground zero, when you are in your courtship period with a military man, things turn amusing from the first day. To begin with, you will suddenly feel more of a nationalist, and the patriotic Hindustani in you will be awakened. As a result, the inexperienced sloppy urban mind will start working earnestly. I saw that stark change in me happening instantly. For example, those exhaustive long debates on news channels with all the fierce reporters charging each other mercilessly had never been on my watchlist before. But soon, they entered my sphere of interest (but only till I got married). Also, the stereo in my car played deshbhakti songs; my every gaze halted at the sight of our national flag on major crossings, buildings, or signals. Even during weekend movie binging, I would choose to opt for military movies. And when the intensity of heavy-duty patriotic dialogues got mixed with the sweetness of the chilled cola I kept sipping throughout, my heart rate could only be brought down with those gentle, intense, long phone calls.

The next morning, I returned to my newly found role of being patriotic. I felt more responsible as a citizen, and from the smallest – like the potato peels my neighbour threw under the tree, to the cigarette butts lying along the staircase of my building – to more significant issues like the latest in world politics and the negligence that led to ice melting in Antarctica, I felt deeply for my country and the world. I believed my better half was a superhero working to fix all of this, and I wanted to support him and make this world a better place for everyone.

After all, love makes you do all sorts of stupid things!

Also, usually, when you are in a relationship with a military man, the neurons in your brain work in a manner that makes you always bring the best out of you. As a matter of fact, when you are with a man and not a boy, you want to behave more like a lady and less like a girl.

One of the first few changes started happening in the closet where a part of my carefree heart had resided with a collection of high-waist, medium-waist, and low-waist jeans – straight-cut, boot-cut, and skinny. It (the heart, not the closet) suddenly underwent a heart transplant and started thumping to desi beats. I started following people like Gayatri Devi and liking pages on Indian handloom. The tattoos on my arm looked less appealing than the bindi on my forehead. The fashion icon in me underwent such a major change that if I were to walk a ramp, the before-and-after appearances would contradict each other like Sabyasachi models versus Met Gala icons.

Also, while living in a metro city where one-third of my life was spent on roads driving back and forth, the meaning of words like 'punctuality' got majorly overhauled from the one mentioned in Oxford dictionaries, and a more evolved and adapted meaning took its place. Especially in New Delhi, punctuality means something different at different hours of the day. At probably 6 to 8 a.m., luckily, it means the actual driving time; from 9 to 11 a.m., it means you can add two to three hours' delay; from 12 p.m. to 4 p.m., again, that delay can stretch between one to two hours because of the unending mammoth work of constructing metro stations, or because of the traffic chaos created by a flat tyre or because a few people thought of jumping non-operational traffic lights at the same time, creating a gridlock.

But during our courtship period, I understood clearly that punctuality in the army means much more than what is written in dictionaries. When a time is set for an event, one has to adhere to it come what may. It's a matter of life and death. And just in case the seniors arrive before you, it definitely means death! Unlike in the army, popular civilian reasons for being late, such as the famous '*dadaji ki maut*', '*chachaji ke bete ki saale ki shaadi*', or '*bete ka mundan*' or '*kitni traffic hai*' don't work. And just in case such wild ideas ever strike anyone's mind to use as an excuse for being late, more experienced peers will advise you to bury it so well that even the mind that created the excuse forgets that it could be so creative. (That was just some friendly advice from a now more experienced army wife.)

The word 'punctuality' is related to the word 'timing'. While in the army, their relationship is like that of a 'maa-beti', in civilian life, it's more like 'saas-bahu'; though in the army, the bahu has succumbed to the mighty saas and now has to make this relationship look like 'maa-beti'. Too confusing! The crux is, punctuality holds a lot of meaning in the army. If the timing of pressing the trigger is late even by a second, the outcome can be something no one even wants to dream of! That is the real reason why the idea of being punctual and understanding the concept of timing is clear to all faujis. It's almost a cliché now, as is most commonly said: '*Fauji hai, to time pe hi aayega*!'

Well, when someone has this level of clarity about time and punctuality, you can imagine the pressure it builds on the other partner who lives in a metro and has her own urban concept of timing. But then, I had that healthy desire in me to put my best foot forward. The never-say-die attitude in me surged, and I was prepared to take it head-on!

But alas! I lived in Delhi, and when the whole city had been dug up for the metro lines, my challenge was to beat the traffic and reach on time – not once or twice, but always. After all, I had been my school's house captain and was always punctual (sometimes even on school holidays!). So, getting back to the plan, I would get ready at 4 p.m. for dinner, drive for two hours in traffic, arrive at the restaurant at 6 p.m., and wait, sipping lemonade with extra ice cubes for the next two hours until it was dinner time at 8 p.m. Finally, I would receive my fauji guest in town and thus prove to him that the lady knows the concept of punctuality and time!

With this and more situations to follow in the coming days, our relationship finally got sealed for life.

Days passed, months passed, and with 'time', I became more experienced and amusingly realized that there are some side effects to falling in love with a military guy. The urge to sort out the world, which began at the start of the relationship, only increased in military company. I started noticing, and sometimes even passing stern looks at, those who sped while changing lanes on roads, colleagues who borrowed my pens and markers but never bothered to thank me or return the same, and even at night, I began staying more alert to see if the chowkidar was doing his duty properly. Sometimes I caught him smoking a bidi, sitting comfortably under a tree on a moonlit night while I was taking my mandatory after-dinner stroll (in anticipation of staying fit and in shape like the man in my life). I gave that unconcerned chowkidar a long, intense morale lecture. Later, he confided in me that I reminded him of his masterji from the village school, who lectured him in the same way I did – to study and work hard in life, or else he would become a chowkidar one day. He further wiped his face and admitted that he never listened to his masterji and was always busy stealing his bidis from his jhola. When I reminded him of his duties like his masterji once did, he thanked me for enlightening him, and with all conviction said, '*Madam, humare colony ko aapke jaisa hi madam log chahiye!*' (Madam, our colony needs women like you!) I took that as a compliment and went back home, thinking, little did the man know that the madam he was talking to would soon be a memsahib. Together with the man of her dreams, they would make the difference this country needed! Listening to '*Chak De India*', I walked back towards my building, enjoying the moonlit night and dreaming of the purposeful days ahead in my life. I surely didn't want to wait!

Now, after more than thirteen years of marriage, when I look back, I feel as if I once lived in a Karan Johar movie. These days, age demands that I just relax, munch on popcorn, and enjoy my cola, leaving the drama for the younger bloods. But *kya karein*! The fauj has kept my josh factor so well-lubricated that I've decided to keep the drama alive forever. After all, age is one thing, and growing up is another!

3

Fauji Love Blues

When you agree to catch up with a partner for dinner dates, it's common for lovebirds to put their best foot forward. Each person keeps no stone unturned in their efforts to impress the other. There's an innocent competition between the two to establish themselves in their partner's mind. This active contest is what nurtures a twenty-century relationship.

In my case, however, the competition was anything but ordinary. The man I chose to date wore a uniform! He would be more willing to put his life on the line at the directive of his commanding officer than for me. He drove a car and a tank with equal efficiency and, above all, loved to wake up at 4 a.m. Initially, the bar to impress seemed beyond my reach. But then, the never-say-die belief in me took over, bolstering my confidence through constant inner monologues, such as, 'You are an independent woman living in Delhi,' 'You

Civilian, hunh, all of you are out of uniform

have your work, friends,' and 'You survive in this city full of competition, which is not everybody's cup of tea.' It finally sounded achievable, and I realized it was better that way when I needed to date a military man whose composed, sorted, organized, and calm demeanour was intimidating for a twenty-five-year-old like me.

It was far from normal for me to see someone my age so restrained with emotions and formal in his dealings, when on the other hand, the rest of my twenty-five-year-old friends were busy dancing, slurping dinner, and asking their girlfriends to pay off their bills because they had spent their entire salary on cigarettes and internet debt. But I set aside these differences and moved forward in my relationship because deep down something about him impressed me every day.

I chose to meet at fancy but gentlemanly restaurants where food was served to the ladies first and the bill presented to the men, where ballads and jazz play softly, and where fork and knife on a plate has meaning. Finding such a place in Delhi was no easy task when you are twenty-five years old on a limited budget and without any helpful suggestions from friends who dine at dhabas, dipping their fingers in butter-chicken curry while shaking a leg to Punjabi pop music.

Soon, I realized that I wasn't the only one in the relationship striving to leave an impression. I sensed that my military partner was grappling with similar challenges in our relationship. I noticed a peculiar aspect of him: even when he was in his best civilian mode, trying to impress his love through fashion, it was tough for him. After all, when someone spends 24/7, 365 days a year clad in olive greens, with a belt so tight it squeezes internal organs, and a haircut so short that even the eyebrows look longer, it can be difficult to adjust.

I understood his challenges, and whenever we met outside the cantonment gates, this olive-green fashionista would, without fail, follow a colour scheme and display every shade of blue imaginable. On the few lighter days when he chose to experiment a bit more, the pattern would change from plain colours to stripes or checks, but his loyalty to the blues was unwavering. This was especially apparent when, one day, I observed the aesthetics of his bachelor room. I was stunned to see his fascination with this hue: a baby-blue gel toothpaste with a darker blue toothbrush, azure-blue shaving gel, ice-blue prickly heat powder with lavender fragrance (please mind that lavender flowers also have a tinge of blue) all neatly lined up, perfectly straight, properly wiped and sparklingly clean as if ready to march from one corner of the shelf to another.

Further into the room, I noticed a powder-blue lampshade with turquoise-blue flowers, a navy-blue bedsheet with a royal-blue quilt and above it a painting of a peacock in Mhow, a military station near Indore, which is also considered the Mecca of art in the Indian Army, and that peacock obviously was painted in peacock blue, with serious eyes looking straight at me as I stood frozen, holding a glass of blue lagoon mocktail offered by the military mess staff, who to my surprise was wearing mufti (a blue uniform for men in ranks). Just then the military man emerged from his changing room, looking dashing in his blue shirt with a Turkish-blue scarf and sapphire-blue cufflinks. I was zapped and quietly gulped down the blue lagoon, sitting on the military sofa with blueprints on it.

But soon after the initial 'healthy competitions' to impress and 'show off' our achievements, from choosing restaurants to fancy meals to the farce of displaying our interest in world politics, we had to come back to reality. And the landing was made smoother by the true love and genuine appreciation of our relationship.

Someone has rightly said, 'Simplicity carried to an extreme becomes elegance.' And that is what I felt and learned from being with a military man. It's not important to brand yourself in fancy clothes and cars when your character speaks volumes for you. And that character is not built by one event; it is the outcome of numerous challenges, especially for a military person. And it is etched so deep in them that, even in their deep sleep, when I observe their posture closely, it is tightly held with arms properly tucked around the chest. Even the tip of the leg won't cross the virtual Line of Control (LOC) of the bed. That is the level of commitment and clarity of mind they possess.

4

The Third Course (Mate) in a Two-course Meal

When you are in a relationship with a military man, you will feel out of this world. You will feel all your fairy tales come alive when the prince charming you have read about comes one day in shining armour and saves you from the atrocities of the world. His gentlemanly qualities will sweep you off your feet, and you will be ready to dive deep into this love that you have read about only in legends and epics, seen only in films. But as you go deeper into this relationship, you will realize there is one bond in his life that you can never replace, and that is the chemistry with his course mates, or 'Bhais' as they lovingly call each other.

A true military man will never be comfortable even if your elbow touches his in public. He will maintain a safe distance and generally sit with straight arms and crossed legs, the epitome of gentlemanly qualities. And to add to this bag of qualities, he will occasionally smile and speak softly and politely, which can be a major challenge for urban ears used to people and traffic hollering.

Even the long, intense courtship phone calls will abruptly end if they go too late into the night as a focused military man will prioritize his morning duties or physical training ritual. So, beyond midnight, no matter what level of emotional turbulence you experience, if it is not life-threatening, cut the call and sleep it off.

However, this enchanting, celestial image turns 180 degrees the moment he meets his sweethearts – his course mates, the eternal haddi in your relationship with him.

These are the friends who have completed military courses together; some of them have been together from their days in the NDA, some from IMA, and some from other military courses that take place throughout their military careers. They have shared the 'best days of the academy' together, shared bikes, food, booze, clothes, books, and even girlfriends at times.

They can forget anyone else in a moment. The whole poised demeanour disappears within a matter of seconds. The glow in their eyes will remind you of Gulzar's line '*Hamne dekhi hain un ankhon ki mehkti khushboo*'. Their laughter will bring back memories of '*Telephone dhun mein hasnewaali*'. They can sit anywhere – on the ground, floor, car's bonnet, and eat anything you offer, whether half-cooked chicken or Maggi. Everything is immaterial in the face of the love they have for each other.

You can feel the energy they radiate when they meet; their hugs and embraces have an uncanny spirit, and for a moment, anyone watching this 'milan' is transported to the celestial milan of Ram and Bharat in the Ramayana where the two brothers met and wept. I am sure, after the profound mention of this intensely emotional brotherly moment, Valmiki too must have struggled to bring the story back to Ram and Sita. I am just a humble mortal soul, so I choose to quietly fold my hands in peace and let this love be.

5

Wedded to the Olive Greens

The trend of hiring wedding planners in Indian weddings has come into vogue over the last two decades; before that, this major event was left to the devoted extended family, majorly consisting of all the mamas and chachas. Though they added a lot of '*apnapan*' in planning these functions, things became more sorted and less dramatic after the wedding planners took over this responsibility. It cut down the hurdles of emotional obligations, and decisions were taken more pragmatically. I support this change, but I also feel many areas in an Indian wedding have a lot of scope for improvement and require a professional touch to simplify issues that tend to go out of hand during weddings. For example, if we had a psychological lesson-plan or a crash course for the entire groom's family on how to emotionally handle an Indian bahu who leaves everything and adopts a new family, or a written exam for all the relatives to qualify before attending a wedding, just imagine the benefits.

I also strongly feel that, besides this, a tutorial is highly recommended for families who don't have the budget to hire wedding planners, so that they can learn to haggle. These vendors, be it the *phoolwallah*, *ghodiwallah*, or *tentwallah*, clearly know that in our country, the planning of a daughter's wedding starts from the day her umbilical cord is cut. They know very well that *ladki ke papa ne bank mein aur maa ne tijoriyon mein save kar hi rakha hoga*. (The girl's father must have saved money in the bank and her mother must have saved it in safes.) They would also be aware of all the filmi emotional dialogues to blurt at the right moments, especially when the young bride finalizes the design of her lehenga and the salesman has succeeded in making her feel like Katrina Kaif. After that, there is no chance of a rebate of even 50 paise. They will make sure it is bought at the highest rates using their umpteen marketing skills.

This is not just marketing, it's an art, an art crafted to a level that even the marketing gurus in Oxford or Harvard can't decipher. The Lajpat Nagar university of sales and marketing masters it all. Now, in such circumstances, when I was roaming around clueless for my wedding shopping, I had to be well prepared, first, because I had limited money in my coffers; second, because I never wanted to splurge; and finally, as always, I believed in '*chhote packet main bada dhamaka*'!

While I was in the process of finalizing the wedding programme, I settled on an elegant golden card with no studs and no extra creativity on the designs. It was a sober piece that appealed to me, and I presumed that it was too simple a card for the flamboyant, gaudy shop, and therefore I expected a discount. However, I happened to meet the wedding invitation *cardwallah* at the counter, and he had no intention of falling prey to my marketing strategies.

He was a seasoned Lajpat Nagar entrepreneur, and the experience he held of the market could be seen by the size of his belly and the amount of chhole kulche stuffed in it from one season of wedding to another. He did not even bother to blink his eyes and waste his energy to fight my flimsy marketing tricks. He looked stoned, bored, and it seemed the only spice left in his life was the green chilly aachar which came complimentary with the plate of chhole kulche he was gobbling down for his lunch.

I felt disheartened, with all my hopes of cracking the deal on my terms and conditions evaporating, when like a sudden shooting star in the sky bringing luck, the name of my fiancé, the military man, came as a saviour.

The cardwallah sitting on the other side of the table accidentally read the message to be printed on the wedding card. His eyes glued to it, all his sluggishness vaporized exactly like the bubbles in the chilled cola he offered me from under his table. With a smile, he asked, '*Captain Sahib ki shaadi hai, aapne pehle nahin bataya.*' (Why didn't you tell before that it is our captain's wedding?)

Little did I know that 'army' is one word in India that unites the whole nation, and no matter how corrupt or business-minded one may be, when one knows one is dealing with someone protecting the borders, the honesty and the truth with which one is naturally born come alive. It's almost like the situation when you are in front of God in a temple, and no matter how many lies you've spoken or how much you've negotiated with the flower vendor outside to get the cheapest pooja thali, when you stand in front of the Almighty with folded hands, it's the purest form of you. Similarly, in our great country, the pedestal of love, respect, and belief on which an army personnel and his family are placed is incredible!

I finally had the wedding card finalized at the desired rate and also enjoyed the free cola and plate of the famous chhole kulche of Lajpat Nagar with the cardwallah bhaiya.

With each day, I started realizing the fact that marriages in our homes are very different from what we see in the movies. The boiling pot of confusion created by hundreds of relatives adding their versions of rituals and preferences can sometimes lead to a lot of muddle-headed decision-making. The problem is exacerbated if the husband-to-be is a military man who may be posted to some hinterland where, forget telephonic calls, even the dropping of rations depends on the mood of the clouds. So he might be simply not available for any pre-wedding discussions. But as they say, a life without challenges, hardships and purpose is pointless. So no matter how much confusion there is, Indian weddings are, hands down, some of the most entertaining affairs in one's life.

Normally, in families where the bride and groom are part of the entire planning, the events are more or less synchronized. The bride and groom are often dressed in colour-coordinated attire, with the lehenga matching the achkan of the groom.

Events like mehndi and sangeet involve fun, frolic, and dancing to dhols and Bollywood songs. Recently, an added feature has been the pre-wedding shoot at beaches and hilltops, with the latest Hollywood songs playing in the backdrop. It looks like a teaser for an upcoming romantic movie. Some humble couples, who choose to save a few thousand, hire a video editor at a discounted rate, though this often leads to quality issues. After the careless edits and use of pirated filters on the faces of the bride and groom-to-be, relatives might be utterly confused on the actual wedding day, unable to recognize the couple from the WhatsApp forwards in their family groups. Nevertheless, with this latest addition comes the pre-wedding grooming package for the extra glow and radiance, which almost matches the glow in the edited pictures. Thus, the couple look bright and shining for the final event. These weddings are near-perfect, cinematic, and seem like a dream come true for the couple. But those are for the aam jodi. Fauji ones live by different rules.

And so, I, supposedly a bride in the next few days, looked haggard and bewildered, all alone. The military man was not available for any decision-making. And expecting him to avail of a last-minute leave to plan his wedding? Perish the thought. It could amount to abandoning his men. Therefore, I had to make peace with the fact that he would at least be present for his own wedding (as he promised), and move on.

Up until the last day, I was negotiating with the caterer for an extra plate of vegetarian food and an extra chaat counter for the evening of the wedding. This was primarily for three reasons: first, I was a prudent bride; second, the husband-to-be was perpetually inaccessible; and third, the memsahib-to-be (i.e., me) was well-versed with the dwindling coffers of a government employee. So, I planned to anchor the sinking ship and save some banknotes that could be used to buy dinner sets and candles once we set up our home.

Our clothes were coordinated in the hope that they would match. Knowing his preferences (and his love for the shade of blue!), I finalized most of the trousseau in similar hues of blue. My nights were long and busy. I edited the pictures we took the last time we met, using my laptop and instructions on editing tools from Google. I exploited the search engine so much that by the weekend, I was planning to make a small teaser to satisfy my urban desire to announce my wedding to my peers. From creating the list of milni malas required to asking the DJ what song to play during the bride's entry, I was involved in everything. The Sardar DJ had the cheek to tell me, '*Mera discussion ho gaya hai bride se, unhone bata diya hai konsa gaana play karna hain.*' (I have discussed it with the bride, and she has told me which song to play.) That will tell you that I looked anything but a bride-to-be. I gave him a stern look and confronted him, saying, '*Shaadi meri hai, bhaiya. Kis bride ki baat kar rahe ho? "Din Shagna Da" song le aana, aur jab main aaoon toh play kar dena. Nahin toh payment usi bride se le lena jis se baat hui thi.*' (This is my wedding, brother. Which bride are you talking about? Please bring the song "Din Shagna Da", and play it when I arrive. Otherwise, collect the payment from the bride you discussed it with.)

I wanted it to be perfect because, no matter what, being in this relationship with the military man, I was beginning to understand one thing clearly: happiness is a choice, not a circumstance.

Finally, just like the way the police in Hindi films enter at the last moment when the lead actor has already resolved everything, the military man arrived for the wedding after all the decisions – from the *shaadi ka ladoo* to the *shaadi ka tattu* – had been made and settled.

No matter how many diamonds or how much pomp and splendour adorn the ceremony, nothing shines better than a military marriage. With all the pomp and circumstance, the memsahib-to-be is made to feel on top of the world. Even the walk to the wedding stage, escorted by military bagpipers playing regimental, thumping tunes, transports you into another world. The modest walk down the aisle feels more like a march with a floral garland in hand, the head held high in pride.

Unlike major civilian events, which get instantaneously flashed on social media at the speed of light, with 1000 likes hitting your pictures before you can blink, the only "social" account a military man has is his government salary account with the SBI. And that account certainly doesn't require any of your fancy photos. All that is needed is a clean-cut couple photo with a blue background so it can be transferred into a joint salary account, which, over the years, transforms into a pensionable account – one silver lining in every military man's life. Thus, there is no need to be weighed down by the baggage of external validation.

And so, finally, with the blessings of our elders, friends, neighbours, vendors, chowkidar, chhole bhature aunty and uncle, coursemates, peers, seniors, the DJ, and every soul who was part of our very soldierly courtship period, we solemnized our relationship into the sacred bond of marriage, which in India is believed to last not just this birth but the next seven births. And with that, my wish to be an army wife for the next seven births too was fulfilled.

6

Trial by Fire

When one has to live in tough terrains and complex work environments with limited resources, work round the clock, deal with tough seniors, and no internet, one makes special efforts to remain light-hearted. That is why fun and frolic in social life have been given equal importance in the army. For newly wedded couples that can take various forms as I would find out.

From the moment the *saat pheras* were completed in the mandap, a conscious effort was made by my husband's battalion to make the first few weeks memorable. I got baptized. Hereon, I would be enjoying some formal titles and would be referred to as ma'am / memsahib or Mrs [Husband's Name]. I also became an 'aunty' for all the military kids from that moment, regardless of some of them being a few years younger than me.

Gajar ka halwa as team-building exercise

Apparently, the welcome of the new bride in the military is completely unlike the initial days a bride outside cantonment walls might experience. The aam bride is not supposed to enter the kitchen till the '*hathon ki mehndi*' has come off. She is pampered and her comforts take priority. She is taken around the new city, fed in fancy restaurants, gifted and blessed by relatives, and always given more than her husband. In contrast, in the army, she would definitely be asked for more than her husband though for different reasons.

Interestingly, from the moment the military man gets married, back in the battalion he belongs to a parallel plan is set in motion. The key planners are the juniors (officers below your husband's rank), ladies (wives of other officers), and the jawans who are so used to obediently follow orders that they will never show the slightest change in their emotions howsoever outlandish the order is. His trained mind is very clear on 'following the order'; the source and nature are irrelevant.

Now, this welcome of the memsahib into her husband's battalion is not some random affair where the puja thali awaits with kumkum and chawal and you get a laddoo in the end. This welcome is made memorable for any lady in the Indian army and let me tell you, no stone is left unturned. It's planned so extensively that a convoluted Manmohan Desai Hindi film couldn't create such intricate plans even if it wants to. However, there's always the likelihood that a military couple wishing to avoid such traps may change the routes they take to reach the station, and won't share their travel details. We tried to be one of them.

Right after the marriage and the mandatory rituals and a trip to the beaches of Goa, it was time for the military man to return. Unaware of what lay ahead, I was carefree and excited to join my newly minted husband and set up my home. Little did I know that the mother of all rituals was waiting for me.

On the night we boarded the train (the nearest airport was a 1000 km away) and left my Karma Bhumi, Delhi, for my Dharma Bhumi, where my husband was posted, I was totally calm. We chatted for a while on the train and then, finally, tired of following all the formalities with the newly found bunch of relatives, I decided to retire for the night. I snuggled comfortably in a Bharatiya Railway cushioned seat and quickly fell asleep. At the stroke of midnight, I heard someone screaming continuously in our bogey: 'Sir! *Kahan ho*, sir?' (Sir! Where are you, sir?) I tried to make sense of what was happening by peeping uncomfortably out of the blanket. I then heard it again, and this time it called out a name that sounded familiar. My husband stood and smiled at me, confirming that it was him they were calling for!

Soon, our stuff was put down on the railway platform and we found ourselves standing there in the midnight cold while our train passed by. I was totally baffled by the situation; it made no sense to me, but the military man knew what lay ahead.

At around an hour past midnight, we were transported to the battalion which was a two-hour drive from the railway station. At the battalion another group of officers was waiting for me in the mess garden. They welcomed me and straightaway asked me to prepare tea for all of them on a stove.

Luckily, I have been an adventurous soul since childhood and out-of-the-box stuff has always appealed to me. I have had the fun of lighting a stove, cooking in jungles, running after rabbits, and throwing cats into buckets full of water all my childhood. Finally, all that was coming to my rescue. I wondered what my mom would make of this moment, as she always accused me of being the mischievous kid of the family.

So, I lit the stove, took the patila, and made tea for the entire battalion. These executors are merciless and they can go to the limits, so the next challenge thrown at me was to cook a complete meal for about forty individuals on a chulah with bare minimum help. They also demanded gajar ka halwa, for which I had to grate a sack full of carrots. I smiled and took up the challenge.

The process started around 6 a.m. I was almost near the finishing line by noon, despite the multiple tea sessions in between for the guests, basically the junior officers, who were sent to me with the sole intention of bugging me. Everything concluded with a few more rounds of such agni parikshas like kissing the frog and singing a hundred deshbhakti songs before I was formally welcomed in the battalion mess for the evening dinner with such dignity and respect that I almost felt like a queen.

After the delightful dinner with friendly chatter, my husband and I were transported to the best guestroom in the battalion and we thought that was the end. However, it was just the beginning of another round of agni parikshas. The key planners for this were the younger bachelor lot of the unit who, in their full josh to disturb the sleep of the newlyweds the whole night, had hidden about twenty alarm clocks inside the room, which, from midnight, kept playing bhakti songs to provide us with some spiritual awakening on the very first day of our life as a married couple in the unit.

After every hour, the alarm clocks would ring, followed by a series of bhakti songs. Not just that, they had a speaker too in our room, which was connected to theirs, and loud announcements were made the whole night, like – '*Sona hai to jag jaao*', '*Jaagte raho*'. My favourite was '*Big Boss ke ghar main apka sawgat hai*'.

I was thoroughly enjoying the moment and finally, when my husband realized that I was coping with all this in the right spirit, he declared, 'You will be a good army wife; I can see that positive military josh in you already!'

I smiled back wondering, what a life I had signed up for!

7

What's in a Name?

How exhilarating is it to hold a tub of popcorn in one hand and a can of chilled cola in the other, watching Tom Cruise glide effortlessly from an aircraft, looking dapper in his Air Force uniform, gelled blonde hair and dark aviators to go with his handsome face perfectly on the big 50-foot silver screen. Also, every time he is addressed as Lt. Pete in the movie, one feels a sudden adrenaline rush. And though good looks do matter, there is also a certain magic in the armed forces' titles and uniforms, which leave a deep impression, particularly on women.

But reality is different! In our society, we love messing around with names and adopting a desi, *chhota-pyaar-se-bhara* title for almost everyone in the family. So, every Siddharth is someone's Sidhu, every Rakesh someone's Rakha, the youngest of the family will be baptized with the universal title of being

Fitting in, standing out

the chotu of the family, the tallest will be called Lambu! So on and so forth.

We all have such names floating in our list of close friends and family. The issue that arises here is that when one grows up in such a relaxed, informal, and natural Hindustani household, it is not easy to adopt a different habit, especially if it is English in nature.

One of my initial tussles being an army wife pertained to remembering names and titles. I used to always mix up the ranks. Terrified that I would cause major embarrassment for both my husband and me in case I ended up referring to the seniors wrongly, the military man took up the responsibility of giving me induction classes to get me attuned to the norms of the army.

So, on a bright sunny Sunday morning, my classes began with a cup of tea in hand under a big neem tree in our garden.

I was told about the trick of referring to an officer without actually remembering his name. My husband looked very different in his civilian clothes. It's not usual for me to see him dressed that way in casual clothes and chappals. But no matter how casual the clothing was, the tone was absolutely sombre and the instructions as crisp as a soldier's march.

He said, as if commanding his battalion, 'So, it's very simple. The first stage involves quickly identifying the rank by observing the number of stars and Ashokas they carry on their shoulders. Thereafter, swiftly look for the nameplate they wear on the right side of their uniform and there you go, you will see the name on it. If you see three stars, it's captain, followed by his first name on the nameplate. If you see one star and one

Ashoka, it's lieutenant colonel, followed by his first name on the nameplate. If you see only one Ashoka, you refer to him as major, followed by his first name. If you see two stars and one Ashoka, it's colonel, followed by his name.'

By now I was more or less seeing stars in broad daylight!

I interrupted, 'What if I see two Ashokas and one star?'

My husband gave a serious look and said, 'No, you will never see that; there is no such rank.'

To this day I have not understood the logic behind having two stars but not having two Ashokas, but then I left that discussion there and moved into my newly formed kitchen to make the mandatory Sunday brunch of rajma chawal.

Over the next weekend, we got an invite for a formal dinner at a mess. I was busy deciding what to wear and which jewellery would match my outfit. Soon, my me-time was interrupted by an unexpected call from my husband, who would not generally call at that hour of the day. Baffled to see his office number flashing on the screen, I picked up the receiver and answered anxiously, 'Hi! How come you called at this hour of the day, sab theek hai na?' I had by now learned that surprises are not always pleasant, therefore, I wanted to confirm everything was alright.

My husband replied, 'Haan haan, all fine! Just wanted to remind you about the dinner we have to attend tonight. Hope you have done your revisions? Remember na? What does two stars and one Ashoka mean? You remember?'

I replied with complete conviction, 'Of course! And I don't need to revise, don't worry I will sail through it! Just chill!'

In the evening, both of us dressed up for the event: me in my bright sari from the wedding trousseau and he in his ceremonial uniform. We took some pictures for memory's sake and then moved to the function.

Now, there is this practice (which I have only recently understood) prevalent in the armed forces whereby senior officers and ladies love to interact with newly commissioned officers and the new brides. They like to know how the new bride feels about being in the army and try to give a bigger picture of the organization. Probably, it's also their way to make newcomers comfortable in the folds of the army. This habit can be compared with a civilian setup where the seniors of the house meet the new bride and make her comfortable in the new household (though some might scare her off as well).

The senior lot could identify me by the colour of my sari (a bright orange one with shimmer work, sindoor, and mangalsutra) from a distance. I realized that I probably looked like a plate of chhole bhature among English dishes.

But then I gained confidence with a sip of the red wine I had been nursing for a while. 'After all, I am a new Indian bride and I should be dressed in bright colours,' my inner monologue started, which happens when I start getting nervous.

I swallowed the wine in one glass took a step forward to shake hands with the senior officer.

'So, you are new here? Hope you are enjoying the army?'

I smiled back and opened my mouth to answer, 'Umm…'

I read his name on the right side of his uniform, General Singh … what do I call him? Mr Singh? Singh Uncle? Just then I remembered I had to look for the ranks on the shoulder; yes, I see Ashoka and I see stars and then this? What is this?

Scissors? Or swords? What is this? My husband never told me about this.

Totally confused with the cryptic signage, I blurted out, 'Singh Uncle, it's nice, and I am having a great time here.'

For a moment, he looked at me dumbfounded, and then raised his whiskey glass saying, 'That's what the army is all about. Cheers!' He then took a step ahead and whispered, 'Young lady! By the way, I am General Singh.' With a smile, he moved away to interact with other guests around.

My poor captain sahib, who had rushed to my rescue seeing the general interacting with me, looked aghast but calmed me down realizing that I was petrified with the faux pas I had just made. He said in his usual poised manner, 'It's alright. Some senior officers do look like uncles at times.'

Later at the dinner table, I was seated next to the general, but I chose to keep silent and opened my mouth only to gobble down the food. General Singh could probably sense that I was terror-struck. So, just to lighten up the situation, he made eye contact and said, 'My daughter must be your age.'

I smiled.

He added, 'Her friends too call me uncle.'

I looked back at him, and we both smiled at the situation. It restored my lost confidence, and from then on, it has been a breeze.

While driving back home, my husband could only guess the reason for my happiness, especially after the 'uncle' incident.

He inquired, 'So, I hope Gen. Singh didn't take your class at the dinner table. You looked rather cheerful interacting with him later. Hope he wasn't too upset about you referring to him as uncle, huh?'

To which the awakened army wife in me replied, 'What's in a name? That which we call a rose by any other name would smell as sweet.'

'What?' my rational military husband inquired.

'Sire! It's Shakespeare,' I teased him.

8

Setting up the Dream Home

I do believe that every woman dreams of setting up home after marriage. Many of us nurture this dream for a long time, and generally the inspiration comes from childhood, when we observe our mother decorating the overlooked corners of the home simply yet beautifully.

My earliest memory is of my mother collecting flowers from the garden and placing them at the feet of brass deities, which she used to religiously polish every day. The porcelain lamps, the diyas on the gates, the incense sticks in every room, the freshly washed linen on the bed, the hot food on the dining table with the crockery matching the table cover – she loved doing it all, and I loved following her in complete awe.

I would imitate my mother's actions, and with my set of dolls, I would try to make my dollhouse a cosy, beautiful place where all my favourite dolls and toys could rest. I would put flowers around the dollhouse, create a colourful entrance, use beautiful pieces of small cloth taken from my mother's closet, make a small kitchen with colourful clay food and fruits, and set everything so perfectly that it looked heavenly. I remember those days so fondly.

Such childhood dreams often rest in every girl's mind, and she cherishes these moments throughout her life, regardless of whether she is a homemaker or works in an MNC, as a businesswoman, teacher, designer, or in the armed forces. These are some of the feminine graces that God has bestowed upon women, and we love implementing our ideas, enjoying the celestial boon of imagination and creativity within us, no matter where we are professionally.

Now, with such an omnific urge in my heart, when I crossed the cantonment gates for the first time as the wedded wife of an army officer, I had similar plans. I had already started dreaming about the ambience I would create in my house: the nooks and corners adorned with beautiful things, my kitchen gleaming with shining brass utensils for Indian food, and ceramic dishes for my cakes and puddings. I had saved countless pages and pictures on my phone, and many more items were waiting in the carts of my online shopping apps.

In the army, there is usually a waiting period before a couple is allotted a house. During this time, the family stays in the mess, which is generally furnished with basic comforts in mind. The bedrooms and living room are aesthetically done, with small study corners containing books of different genres, a small tea corner with various teabags, and typically a welcome message from the commanding officer to make you feel more comfortable and welcomed. The mess staff usually asks about your meal preferences and serves them hot and on time. Often, these mess stays are quite comfortable, and they come with a deep realization that life can be simple with minimal things and basic amenities. One feels uncluttered and uncomplicated in every possible way. Not only is it simple, but the right amount of elegance and class is infused into every little thing. Moreover, during this period, when someone is newly posted or joins the battalion with his wife for the first time, as per army traditions, all the other married officers invite them for dinners and coffees at their homes. This also makes the newcomers feel comfortable and cared for.

This happened to us too. We were quite new to the station and were waiting for our house to be allotted. During this period, we were frequently invited by fellow officers as a gesture of welcome.

When the invite for the very first such dinner came, I took a deep breath and felt relieved, expecting that I would finally relax, just be myself, wear comfortable clothes, eat pizza, listen to the music of my choice, and sit comfortably on beanbags. After all, that's what house parties are like, right?

But while the party was indeed fun, there was a twist in the story!

All this time, as I visited the houses of our peers, seniors, and juniors as guests, I could clearly see that a lot of effort had been put in by the host. Unlike the house parties I had attended in civilian life, where we ate pizzas straight from the boxes, here I saw a lavish spread of meals and appetizers, which, to my surprise, had been prepared by the lady of the house. The host also went the extra mile to make us comfortable by constantly engaging in pleasant conversation and making us feel at home. This was a stark contrast to the last house party I attended at a friend's place, where she went off to sleep after a heavy day at the office and asked us to order, eat, and then clean up her house. Here, the lady of the house planned and cooked food according to our preferences and was unbelievably warm and welcoming in her conduct.

Seeing all this, my internal monologue began: 'How are they managing all this? After so much cooking, how do they still have the energy to attend to us?'

I observed that they would stick to conversations on common topics and were eager to hear about our experiences before marriage. Very subtly, they would also make me aware of the sacrifices and responsibilities of an army wife. The moment they realized the conversation was getting serious, they would immediately lift the mood by humorously talking about the perks and privileges.

By now, I was beginning to understand that the army was not just about combat, risk, and war planning; rather, it is a life of deep fulfilment, both professionally and personally. The whole system rests on a perfect cohesion of integrated values, camaraderie, traditions, elegance, patience, and much more, which I was in the process of experiencing.

Besides the warm welcome, the food, and the conversations, what drew my attention and amused me no end was the way the interiors were done in their fauji house. I complimented the lady of the house on her amazing taste: 'Your house looks out of this world, very elegant, I must say.'

The lady of the house smiled while holding a platter of cheese, berries, and multigrain crackers. I took a piece, and then she said, 'You see, the point to notice here is that all the houses in the army have similar layouts until your husband makes general, and probably by then, you won't have as much interest in these household affairs. So, set up your house nicely now, invest in it, let your properties be seen and not locked away in bank coffers.'

I thought, now someone was talking sense! After all, I've always believed in 'Zindagi na miley dobara!' But then she added, 'On the flip side, always think prudently. Your husband is a government employee, so invest wisely in your home. But luckily, these architects have really taken care of fauji bank accounts. If you get a set of curtains made now for your first home, rest assured that they will fit the windows of all the fauji houses you move into throughout your husband's military career. These curtains have been with me for the last fifteen years, and these carpets were passed on to us by my mother-in-law, who retired ten years ago. She bought them in the 1970s from Kashmir. That's the magic of these houses, so plan well and trust the system. It will take care of us in all possible and sometimes in the most unimaginable ways.'

Saying this, she picked up the same platter with cheese, berries, and multigrain crackers. This time, I picked a piece of cheese, put it in my mouth, which melted instantly, while I observed the ancient curtains and carpets and remembered the quote, 'Cheese is milk's leap toward immortality.' For now, I might as well be satisfied with that piece in my mouth.

However, this bounty of having similarly patterned houses comes with unfortunate coincidences, which I witnessed at the dinners that followed.

I observed that since the layout of all the houses was generally similar and the shopping options for furnishing these spaces were limited due to the cantonment being in some far-flung, isolated back of beyond, the ladies had only one or at most two shops in the local market to pick up household items. As a result, it was common for one item to match with another in someone else's house.

I found it amusing that the curtains of one home matched the sofa upholstery of another, and the cushion cover of this home matched the dining sheet of that. The similarities didn't stop there; they ranged from matching pots and plants to paintings, dinner sets, candles, table mats, curtains, rugs, artificial flowers, and even saris. Everything matched!

Again, the credit for such coincidences definitely goes to the geographical location of the cantonments and the restricted choices they offer. It actually poses a significant challenge to your creative imagination when you have inadequate resources, a circumscribed budget, and a house with a military owner demanding the most exquisite setup.

To top it off, the lush greenery around the house plays a crucial role, harbouring some permanent residents such as squirrels with big teeth who believe in munching on whatever you forget to pick up, and some flying guests like the family of pigeons who always build their palace of dreams above your AC window. Though they do contribute and pay rent by working as full-time alarm clocks, squawking every minute of the day.

A few more creepy guests like to slither around periodically, and some will jump over the fence and purr every time the meat and milk invite them. The humongous tree in the backyard stands tall and looks older than your grandfather, with its deep roots stretching for half a kilometre. To cut a long story short, the wildlife outside, and sometimes inside the house, will keep you engaged throughout, while you struggle to reconcile with the interior guru within.

I concluded from my research that it would require a lot of inner peace to set up a house in this remote location, and let me tell you, all the Instagram photos and videos I had saved for reference definitely had no relevance in this habitat.

It's left to one's own creativity and imagination to build wonders out of shambles. I couldn't take that much stress on my newly wedded soul, so I made a cup of Indian coffee with a generous amount of milk and sugar, took a sip, and opened an old architectural coffee-table book I had with me for a long time. I flipped through the pages and stopped at a picture where I saw what looked like a caveman making a cart. I could relate to that poor fellow and wondered about the hardships and challenges these architects from the time of Adam and Eve must have experienced before they created such masterpieces that still take your breath away.

That day, I understood the real meaning of decorating a house, where instead of splurging, you require skill, creativity, sensibility, and most importantly, 'patience' to bring about a vibe, a character in the house, a quality I had lacked from the beginning.

I actually started feeling like a fighter pilot in a cockpit, completely new to the machine and technology, with no clue as to what to do with it. I knew I would need ample practice, trials and errors, guidance from veterans, and self-confidence to reach that level. With a fresh mind and a positive outlook, I geared up, and soon our first trip to the cantonment was planned.

The regiment received us with warmth and fondness. As newlyweds and the latest to join, we were the stars in everyone's eyes. Our first dinner was planned at our CO's residence, and the invite came in the form of a WhatsApp message. At first, I thought of ignoring it, but soon my husband informed that I had to take the invitation with utmost importance and seriousness, as the CO's house is the most important and coveted residence in the unit.

The CO was a tall, dark man, and with the ever-charming lady of the house beside him, the two looked elegant, sophisticated, and well-spoken. I realized their house was a true reflection of their personalities. The decor was a mix of traditional artefacts, antique furniture, and a dash of modernity. In some way, it represented the army itself – traditions and values with a touch of modernity.

I wasn't much of an antique or vintage fan before marriage, but soon it dawned on me that when a lady marries an officer, the most crucial part is her adaptation to this style, as it reflects the very essence of army life – its history, its bravery, and its valour. I noticed an immaculate room with medals, badges, and commendations framed and displayed in the most refined manner. This was an entirely new setup for me. I was used to fairy lights and IKEA furniture; here, I saw wooden, carved furniture, heavy drapes, brass artefacts, and those swords hung so proudly on the wall! I must admit I got butterflies in my stomach as I realized the challenge I would face in the years to come to create a similar setup in our own house.

Dinner was served in their perfectly manicured garden, which was in full bloom – the roses, lilies, jasmines, fountains, and sculptures all in harmony with the night's breeze.

The conversation was pleasant, full of anecdotes and stories of past experiences. The CO's wife was a gracious host, guiding me through the entire dinner – what to eat, how to eat, and most importantly, what to say. She ensured I was comfortable and at ease throughout the dinner. I understood that she was the backbone of the entire setup, and I had a lot to learn from her. My husband looked happy and proud as he mingled with his peers and seniors. It was a proud moment for both of us, being welcomed so warmly into the regiment. The evening ended with a toast to our future, and we returned home with hearts full of gratitude and excitement for the journey ahead.

The next few days were a whirlwind of activities. Settling into the new house, setting up the kitchen, organizing the living room, and arranging the bedroom to suit our taste. I quickly realized that setting up a house in a cantonment is different from the usual city apartments I had seen or lived in before. Here, everything had a purpose; everything was carefully thought out and planned. There was no space for unnecessary clutter, and every piece of furniture or decor had to be both functional and aesthetically pleasing.

I was fortunate to have the guidance of the senior ladies in the regiment. They were like walking encyclopaedias of army life, with tips and tricks to make the most of the limited resources we had. I learned how to repurpose old furniture, mix and match different styles, and bring life to a room with just a few key pieces. Slowly but surely, our house started to feel like home.

The garden was the next project. It was a small patch of land, but I was determined to make it a little oasis of peace and tranquillity. With the help of a few gardening books and some advice from the local gardener, I started planting flowers, herbs, and vegetables. Every morning, I would spend some time in the garden – watering the plants, weeding the beds, and simply enjoying the fresh air and the sound of the birds. It became my sanctuary, a place where I could unwind and recharge after the day's activities.

The house was finally coming together; it was a mix of our personalities, tastes, and love. It was a place where we could relax, entertain friends, and create memories that would last a lifetime. As I looked around, I couldn't help but feel a sense of accomplishment and pride in what we had created together.

The journey of setting up our first home in the army was not without its challenges, but it was a journey that taught me so much about myself, my capabilities, and the importance of making a house a home. It was a journey that brought us closer together as a couple, as we navigated the ups and downs of army life, learning and growing together. As we settled into our new life, I knew this was just the beginning of many more adventures to come.

The years ahead would be filled with new postings, new houses, new challenges, and new memories. But no matter where the army took us, I knew I had the strength and creativity to turn any house into a home. That was the greatest lesson I learned in my first home. It wasn't about the size of the house, the location, or the furniture; it was about the love, effort, and creativity that went into making it a place of comfort, warmth, and happiness. That was a lesson I would carry with me for the rest of my life, wherever the army might take us.

9

Guests, Gods, Goons

'*Athithi Devo Bhava*' is a concept well known to all Indians; we regard our guests as gods and treat them with whatever best is available. Various folk tales, from Krishna visiting the Pandavas in exile to Sudama meeting Krishna in his palace, strengthen this pious concept of affability towards our guests.

Over the years, traditional value systems have undergone major changes to suit the modern world, marked by a race against time and an aspiration to outpace others. For all the time one is outside the cantonment gates, one exists in a modern and much more advanced social apparatus. In old times, having guests at home meant a week's planning of various purchases from vegetables and fruits to exotic rations, including biscuits wrapped in fancy, colourful covers, fruit jams, and coffee jars. The joy of witnessing all of it come together was not less than any festival. However, in present times, the lack of time and availability of things at the press of a phone button has transformed these old joys. Although the feeling remains the same, the medium has changed. Now, if we have guests coming home, modern phones start flashing discounts on food apps and present varied and attractive options, which might leave Sudama flabbergasted with your hospitality standards.

However, the army remains relatively untouched by this wave of modernity. On Sunday afternoons, while most Indian households follow norms such as husbands making morning tea, couples visiting unisex salons, or planning to watch a movie or order meals from outside, a Sunday in a military house is unpredictable with unusual guests throughout the day.

In a military home, the day often starts with the barber of the battalion ringing the doorbell. For an hour, he will trim the already trimmed hair of your husband, then soak the head with the most pungent-smelling oil (which may come from his remote village) that could be used as chloroform if needed, and then almost break all the bones in his shoulders and back with the champi or massage. You can hear the bones cracking.

The other mandatory Sunday guest will be the gardener, who will come to trim those extra bushes growing in your house (often inside your house too) and then, after the job is done, will discuss his entire horticultural knowledge with the military man, who, to unwind himself and think beyond the army, will spend most of the precious hours of the day with these fellows.

Having your Sunday guests over is one thing; dealing with the expectations they bring is another. Even as my husband comes inside after spending quality time with the Sunday guests, he will ask me, 'Can we offer them something? Maybe a cup of tea and some snacks?'

The snacks in the army are expected to be homemade. 'Homemade' items always takes precedence over everything, even the best meals, in the army. It cannot be emphasized enough. It seems to provide a physiological comfort, as army men are trained to stay emotionally and sometimes physically away from 'home'; anything that reminds them of it is always given the utmost preference.

So, a typical army house will definitely have homemade goodies for the wide range of guests pouring in and out every day, ranging from the *safaiwallah* arriving in the morning to the general saab coming for dinner in the evening. Efforts to make them feel at home are genuinely made, fostering bonds of love and respect.

In the early days in my new home, I experienced having this varied list of guests who, besides enjoying the hospitality, enjoyed the liberty to critically analyse everything I offered from my inexperienced kitchen. I was always under their scrutiny, but the irony is that this attitude didn't make me miss my husband's critical kinfolk.

I believe that such liberties are often a result of the strong bonds we share with each other. Therefore, if the gardener bhaiya rates my 'homemade' halwa below the standards of the halwa made by his mom back in the village using pure ghee and mother's love, I don't mind the sarcastic comments he makes, such as, '*Memsahib, ye diet wala halwa banaya hai*?' (Madam, have you made a diet halwa?). Or if the tasteless cup of English Earl Grey tea I made for my military husband with the purest organic tea leaves my brother got for me from London, results in the following comment laced with as much sarcasm as the roadside tea is with milk and sugar, '*Memsahib, saab ko pure doodh wali chai pilao, ye toh dairy ka hai.*' (Madam, make sure sir drinks tea made of pure milk. Don't use dairy milk.)

I became accustomed to such caustic comments, knowing that they were family. The military man in the house made it clear from day one that, regardless of rank, everyone in the army is a soldier working towards the same cause. I was expected to respect everyone as such, and I was accepted as a family member from the first day.

During one of those early days, in my eagerness to be accepted by 'my new family', I decided to go beyond the expected and showcase my hospitality skills. I peeped out of my window and saw a bunch of men who seemed to have come home to discuss some urgent military matter. Since the military man in the house was busy on an official call, continuously repeating 'sir, sir, and sir' every two seconds, I realized this might take a while.

To keep my guests engaged, and also to flaunt my kindness, I thought of making a strong ginger tea. I rushed to the kitchen, took all the spices that could be added to my special English Earl Grey tea, dipped the teabags generously, and kept options for sugar cubes, honey, and low-calorie sugar sachets stacked properly in different bowls. Soon, I was ready with my English display of tea for my guests. Just to make it more special, I thought, 'Let's take out the fine porcelain cup and saucer set I got as a wedding gift,' from someone I don't even remember or care to remember.

So, finally, the whole spread of tea and homemade snacks was set on a newly bought Fabindia tray, and I walked out holding it firmly to offer it to the bunch of guests still waiting for the military man to finish the call.

'Thank you, memsahib! Thank you, memsahib! Thank you, memsahib!' they all uttered humbly, picking up the cups, saucers, and sugar rather uncomfortably. The disappointment was visible in the innocent eyes of my simple guests, who, although they couldn't say anything verbally, showed through their expressions that they would have preferred a mug full of strong Indian chai with ration *wala tez patti* and ginger over the small portions of fancy tea. I learned a lesson that day, willing myself to transform into a '*pure desi fauji memsahib*'!

I further learnt through my intricate observation skills that the formal dinners at home are some of the most elegantly organized events where the art of an army lady creating wonders using the basics is seen, felt, and deeply admired. For instance, drinks will be served in classy crystal glasses at the right temperature, the tray of snacks will be arranged exquisitely, and the hosts will remain warm and dignified throughout the night, despite having spent the previous hours running around for soda bottles and ice cubes.

Interestingly, besides all the law, order, and discipline, the most popular law in the army is Murphy's Law. I was an arts student, so whenever in fauji parties I heard the reference to Murphy's Law, I ignored it as I had Newton's law of motion in school. But then Murphy's Law in the army is such that no matter what, everyone has experienced and learnt it in some way or another. I understood it in one of the major events I had planned.

Around forty adults, along with children, and nine young officers, who have an unbelievable appetite to devour all your dishes in a matter of seconds, were coming to our home. I had to plan the whole dinner for everyone and that too in military style, which starts with drinks and snacks, before moving on to the main course, desserts, and then with the final round of coffee. While I was wondering in my kitchen where to start, I was faced with the challenge of converting antiquated fauji rations into exotic dishes while dealing with unpredictable power cuts.

I started my spree of cooking, chopping, and at the same time setting the pudding. Now, Murphy's Law came into action. The electricity went out. I had to bake a sponge cake for the pudding, but the cream in the refrigerator started melting instantly. Also, with the power gone, the air fryer wouldn't work for the snacks, and the lamps wouldn't function as the inverter was pulling up the power. Amidst this chaos, I accidentally broke two plates from my dinner set and was now short on plates.

Well, such situations may send any Indian host into a tizzy but in military households they are no match for a seasoned veteran of such circumstances. Little do they know that an army wife is adept at handling all domestic combats. After spending just a few months in the military with my military man, I was no less than a domestic military ninja who knew all the ways and manners to handle unpredictable situations arising in my kitchen, life, or even beyond my boundary of love and care with utmost grace.

Coming back to the disaster in my kitchen, I couldn't have taken a chance with not being able to host my guests properly; that would have been the last thing to even think of. Also, by now I had learnt to perform instant kitchen hacks and create wonders, ensuring my guests didn't get the slightest hint that the situation was out of control.

So, the ninja in me awoke, and I instantly took the bread from the military bakery, chopped the sides, soaked it in sugar syrup, and layered it with whipped malai, which almost did the work of whipped cream. I layered it with custard and fresh fruits, kept it over a vessel full of water, and covered it with a damp cloth. It worked to keep the pudding cool. I also took out a big pan filled with fauji ration *wala namak*, warmed it for a while, and then placed my snacks over another container, covered it for some time, and finally got my snacks baked instead of air frying them. The lamps couldn't be lit because of the power cut, so I lit some fifty candles all over, which provided the perfect ambience I intended to create. The plates were replaced with others from the kitchen rack. After all, it's the love and warmth in your heart, the joy in your eyes, and the friendships you create in life that people truly long for.

We made some lifetime memories that evening. I still clearly remember the happy faces, the nonstop banter, and the unrestrained laughter. And finally, when the guests left, the house looked completely different – with piles of used plates, glasses, and dishes, burnt-out candles, dirty rugs, and floors. It looked completely messed up, but that did not bother me. The vibe in the house felt so positive; the echo of the good times still vibrated through the space. I realized this is the magic of 'Athithi Devo Bhava' – guests leave their magic behind. (Though it took two days for me to set the house back in order.)

10

Master Chefs of Love

No matter how refined your culinary skills are, the army provides enough hungry guinea pigs to its ladies to keep them on their toes. These guinea pigs generally come in the form of the young officers with an unquenchable appetite. They possess this unique quality where their hunger is direct proportional to the amount of bashing they get during the day from their seniors – your husband, for sure! Maybe it's their way at getting back at their senior.

By the way, this is not at all an impulsive outburst emerging from spending an awful day but a quintessential tradition in the army that probably all military husbands have followed with their seniors and ladies. It is taken in good spirit and most of the time works as a bonding factor between the brother officers. The lady acts as a catalyst in this and generally bridges the gaps between the officers. Amusingly, this magic generally lies in her kitchen and the home-cooked food she makes, though at times many creative culinary inventions also take place.

These impromptu do-s are rather unlike the organized dinners we have in army messes where we follow courses of meals and a defined pattern, strict dress codes to adhere to, officers in shining dinner uniforms with the stars sparkling on their shoulders, colourful ribbons on their chests – each colour narrating a different story of a different posting they have earned through their lives – and their radiating nameplates suggesting they are much more than just a name their parents once kept lovingly. Their better halves are elegantly wrapped in classy chiffon or silk saris with pearls strung around their necks and a gleaming pride in their eyes for the man they have chosen. The cutlery is meticulously laid and table etiquette is thoroughly followed.

These formal dinners fatigued me quite a bit, so I often amused myself during such occasions, especially during the long monologues of higher officials. I would begin to correlate such moments in formal dinners with the Victorian era and start feeling as though I were sharing the table with the Queen in Buckingham Palace, with a bagpiper playing around the dinner table while I munched on my food, surrounded by exotic flowers and candelabras. The antique silver cutlery and the band playing regimental songs in the background made my thoughts sail straight to the surreal world of Imperial Britain.

My reverie often broke with the fiery taste of green chilli in the lasagne I had in my mouth, realizing that an overexcited mess cook who had not been briefed a million times to stick to the recipe would try doing his magic, adding a dash of lemon juice in the Russian salad for an extra tang. This often pulled me back from British hypnotism to the reality of Indian cooks.

Coming back to the story, the informal dinners, on the other hand, involve uninvited, ever-hungry pack of young officers who can eat anything in any order. They can start with halwa, have cold coffee with ice cream and extra chocolate, eat aloo paratha with dahi and can easily gulp down hot coffee over it! They would also like to ransack your fridge and stuff themselves with chocolates, cold milk, leftover mithai, malai, dry fruits while they negotiate the dinner menu with you. They would also definitely like to take away the cake you specially prepared for your husband and will add to the agony with promises to come back! The only comforting aspect is that they can eat anything without judging it at all.

Like in traditional India, in the army too, 'food' is not just a meal to fill your appetite. A lot of emotions are attached to it. When a meal is cooked for loved ones, the food not only nourishes their bodies but also assuages them mentally and emotionally. The concept of preparing meals with purity in heart, positive emotions, and immense happiness in the soul has always been there in India from the Vedic eras to modern India and has been passed down from one generation to the next. Interestingly, the flavours of the same dish will vary from one community to another, from one state to another, and also from one family to another. The idea of unity in diversity is felt in our food too.

Now, the concept of food has a lot of layered meanings in the army where it is customary to call each other for dinners, host lunches and breakfasts for peers crossing your town, or send food for the family who recently shifted to your neighbourhood, or for the pregnant lady whose husband is posted elsewhere and left her behind with the faith that the families around will take care of her. The reasons are ample and the love is abundant. When that's the equation, any well-groomed military wife will not leave even a stone unturned.

However, the custom of this ritual also varies with time and the state of mind of an army wife. Initially filled with unbridled enthusiasm, I, who had been married for almost a year, experimented extensively with my culinary skills and tried making recipes I had saved on my phone for a long time. I followed the recipes religiously and bought, with great difficulty due to our remote location, all the branded herbs and spices when I visited a major town. Dishes like three-layered lasagne, stuffed buns, colourful salads, and chia pudding were among my experiments, which I offered to a wide range of guests – from the gardener of the house to my neighbours and the ever-hungry young officers.

Thereafter, soon a stage came in my life when the branded bottles of olive oil, spices and herbs got over and I didn't even bother to replace them. I settled down with the basics in my life; if the guests were treated with a bowl full of dal and sabzi, it was almost luxury. The choices of dishes were based on the seasonal vegetables and precisely what I received last in the ration supply. Also, the pudding was made from unused extra packets of milk piled in the freezer or, if I woke up on the wrong side of the bed, it could be the tinned rasgulla bought from the battalion canteen.

The final category includes the ladies who have been married for over ten years. They are the seasoned lot, having gone through these acid tests so many times in their married lives that now, whether they have bottles of herbs, tins of rasgulla, or nothing at all, they can create masterpieces even with crumbs of bread.

As I write this, I am at that stage of my life and therefore, I can confidently say that I have a supplement of almost everything in my life, or rather, in my kitchen. There are occasions when I have a full supply of electricity and even the ovens and refrigerators are working in full blast, but still, in my state of mental evolution, I prefer not to burden myself with baking a cake, cooling it down, and waiting to make my puddings. Instead, I opt for kitchen hacks like using lemon in cream to curdle it, grating a bit of ginger into digestive biscuits for a ginger biscuit taste, or using crushed cornflakes in chicken to give it a grilled taste like those from KFC. The list of my smart kitchen hacks goes on and on.

The point here is that no matter what anybody has, there is always a choice to embrace responsibility, especially in today's busy modern world where words like tradition and culture hold little esteem. In such times, when similar choices also lie with an army lady, she chooses to be the flagbearer of such traditions. She takes pride in following these traditions, regardless of official commitments, workhour management, and responsibilities for home and family. Yet she still connects the bridges in her world with her nurturing human qualities of compassion, love, and thoughtfulness. She stands tall with her commitment towards the organization. Irrespective of her limitations and no matter what is cooked in her kitchen, it is always a masterpiece. When you have the right intentions and a feeling of abundance in your heart, nothing is ever inconsequential.

11

Battle of the Nine Long Yards

As a child, I often asked my mother who was always clad in colourful, pretty saris, '*Aap ye sari sambhalte kaise ho? Na toh iss mein hook hai aur na hi nada.*' (How do you manage this sari? It has neither a hook nor a drawstring.) This was in the late 1980s when the concept of pre-stitched or ready-to-wear saris did not exist. She would reply with a hearty laugh, and I found the whole idea of wearing a sari utterly farcical and illogical. I wore my comfortable, baggy, stone-washed jeans with Bon Jovi's name finely embroidered on the back pocket, and considered the saree an impractical outfit – something in which one can't jump, run, or cycle. It impedes movement, doesn't have pockets, and above all, has no hook or nada to hold it up! It was too risky for me!

Twenty years later, during one of our early days in the cantonment as a married couple, we received an invitation to

Victory will be ours, one sari at a time

an evening mess function. I read the invite in detail, noting the specified information about the function, for whom and what it was. I carefully read each line, trying to understand the system. Then, I read further, where the invitees' names were written beautifully in calligraphy using black ink. But at a glance, I only saw my military man's name on it, not mine.

'Is this a stag party?' I inquired.

My freshly-minted husband frantically took the invite from me, read it, and replied, 'It's for both of us.'

I looked at the invite again and found myself mentioned as 'Mrs' right after my husband's rank and just before his name. As a young bride, especially one like me who had worked extensively in the civil world and given blood, sweat, and tears to establish my identity, I was riled. 'Am I just a "Mrs" now? Have I lost my name as well, along with everything else I left behind?'

Before I could recover from the shock of the emasculation of my identity as a woman, another awaited me: the last line mentioned the dress code as 'saris' for ladies. A tsunami of emotions filled my heart as I read that word. I instantly remembered my extensive debates with my mother about the impractical aspects of this outfit, how I had skipped Teachers' Day and farewell parties in school just to avoid wearing a sari, feeling I looked like a complete, feeble, wimpy, disoriented woman in that impossible nine yards of cloth. And today, here I was, with the invite in my hand, wondering, '*Kaash! Maa ki baat sun li hoti!*' (Alas! I should have listened to my mother!)

Nevertheless, the fighter in me soon pulled me out of the abyss, and I started digging through my closet for anything remotely resembling a sari. Unfortunately, I found nothing longer or wider than a scarf. At that uncertain juncture, my luck worked (thanks to my mother's systematic, disciplined daily puja with marathons of loud and musical aartis to awaken good-luck charms in our lives). I instantly remembered that, having just married, my suitcases were full of gaudy, shimmery stuff. My buried wedding trousseau came to life as I opened it and pulled out one of the worst fears of my childhood – a bright blue sari with silver stones all over it. Since it had no hook or nada, I knew it would be a waste of time to even try wrapping it myself.

I needed help, so I ran, taking my car to the nearest salon, where they finally pinned it on me using a thousand pins. When I reached the party, I wished terribly for wheels on my shoes to move me from one place to another. It felt impossible to walk, stand, or sit. The Hindi idiom '*phoonk phoonk ke paon rakhna*' acquired a new meaning that evening. I would have never realized the import of that phrase but for the sorry (sari) figure I cut. Throughout the party, I observed the other army ladies around me and the ease with which they carried the nine yards. They wore such beautiful colours and prints that added so much charm to the surroundings. For the first time, I was awestruck by the mystique of a sari, the femininity it endowed on a woman. At that moment, I realized it was never about the sari – it was all about my '*angoor khatte hain*' attitude. I abandoned that mindset there and then, and walked back (with great difficulty) determined to emerge more confident next time.

Within a few days, I went to the market, bought a lightweight chiffon sari, and started practising every day as soon as my soldier left for work. I downloaded the simplest YouTube video on how to drape a sari and followed it through countless trials and tests until finally it all came together. Neatly folded pleats and an elegantly falling palla on the left hand allowed me to walk comfortably and gracefully towards the mirror. Unlike earlier times, it no longer looked as if something was stuck between my knees. I saw myself in the mirror and smiled at the reflection of a lady in me.

The sari fever soon started building up with every compliment I received from friends and family, to whom I sent selfies right before and after attending parties. Additionally, since this was the so-called uniform of army wives, I realized that every season and occasion demanded a different material and colour. Chiffons and light shades were reserved for day or afternoon functions, while crapes and silks were for the evening. Light-coloured saris were for summer and darker ones for winter. Embroidered saris from Kashmir were added to my collection, and a Maheshwari shadow-work sari became a must-have for every army wife. I collected Chanderi saris when posted in Bhopal and silks when in the south. A friend sent me a Mekhla chador, and I bought a few others just because they looked so nice. Chiffons are evergreen and chic, so one in each colour was mandatory. Hand-painted and block-printed saris were also a must. The sari fever kept building up with every posting.

However, building such a sweeping collection is neither a one-day affair nor pocket-friendly. For an army wife, especially, it comes after considerable due diligence. The best time to indulge in such well-considered shopping is during seasonal sales. I often waited with bated breath for summer to end so I could buy a hand-painted chiffon sari in September, knowing that by October, it would be out of season, and silks and crepes would take over.

'*Madam, chiffon kyun le rahe ho? Ye Kanjivaram silk dekho, aaj hi stock Wellington se aaya hai!*' (Madam, why are you buying chiffon? Look at this Kanjivaram silk; it arrived only today from Wellington!) says the sari shop bhaiya, whose outlet lies behind the masjid in the third gali from the chaapwallah's shop, adjacent to the famous dupattewallah's run by two brothers – one who cannot see and the other who cannot speak, but between them they have the world's best dupatta collection. The popularity of these two shops, the sariwallah and the dupattewallah, can be broadly compared to Harrods in London: just as anyone visiting London will go to Harrods whether they buy anything or not, any army wife in our cantonment will visit these shops, whether she buys anything or not.

To add to this, these famous shops are generally located in the most confusing lanes, so finding them is like going on a wild goose chase. Even the GPS gets confused, twirling around in uncertainty. But for an army wife on a mission to buy her favourite sari at a sale price, it's like a whirlwind – a WO(MAN) on a mission, and woe unto the person who stands in the way! Light at the end of the tunnel. *Darr ke aage jeet hain.* Whichever way you put it.

To cut a long story short, when I finally reached the shop, and was asked why I was buying an off-season product when fresh stock was right there, I glanced at the owner sharply, eyebrows raised, and said, '*Bhaiya, off-season mein le rahi hoon. Ab kaun chiffon pehnega? Mujhe to kisi ko gift karna hai, iss liye le rahi hoon. Discount kitna de rahe ho, ye bataao?*' (Bhaiya, I'm buying it off-season. Who is going to wear chiffon now? I'm getting it to gift someone, that's why I'm buying it. So, tell me, how much discount are you offering?)

Thus began the wheeling-and-dealing for the next two hours. Finally, I took my victory march out of the shop, holding the sari I wanted to buy, at a price I could afford. So next time you see an army wife clad in a beautiful sari, standing gracefully, remember this war of the wardrobe!

12

Army-brand Elixirs: Tea and Power Naps

We read in school that rishis and munis used to get up early in the morning during the Brahma Muhurta, take a bath in ice-cold water of a flowing river, and pray to the sun god. Afterward, they would sit on top of a high rock to meditate to attain purity of mind and soul. Such tales are often part of our regular syllabus in school, intended to inspire the new generation and familiarize them with the culture and traditions of the past.

While these tales of disciplined and strict lifestyles sound ideal, they often feel more romanticized than realistic. Now, as urban dwellers, we are used to snuggling in comfortable beds with the luxury of temperature control from the air conditioner buzzing in the corner, and alarms with a snooze button. I wonder who cares about the purity of mind and soul as long as the option of stretching one's morning sleep is available.

Sleep and tea are the two lifestyle comforts every fauji yearns for. These two aspects are deeply ingrained in the Indian Army's culture. The root of this unexplainable affection often lies in the rigorous lifestyle, tough training routines, and adverse climatic conditions in which a soldier is performing his duties. Sometimes his body is half-dipped in snow and he can barely keep himself warm, sometimes he is sitting inside tanks where the temperature nears 50 degrees Celsius, or sometimes inside a thick, wet jungle fighting off leeches and looking for solid ground under the feet. In such adverse circumstances, a short break for the kadak chai made in the battalion kitchen, or langar, boiled to such an extent that it nearly melts the vessel it is made in, with ruthless amounts of sugar and milk which further accentuate the taste, is amrit and ambrosia rolled into one. This concoction boils down into a hot cup of a power drink that tastes far better than a normal cup of tea. When this chai hits the system of any individual in the army, it revitalizes every cell in the body, activating energy in every neuron and proton, readying them for another stretch of diligent work. That is the kind of magic a cup of chai holds for a military person.

Moreover, a lot of memories are built around this cup of joy. A chai break symbolizes a brief respite from relentless duties, offering a moment to stretch, smile, and find comfort before resuming the commitment to the nation.

Ek fauzi ki neend kabhi puri nahin ho sakti. It sometimes seems that even the roosters within the cantonment walls complain of sleeplessness due to the early-morning hustle of military men preparing for physical training and other duties. Observing the volume of tasks conducted during the wee hours in a cantonment, it feels as though another sun has risen for them hours before it does for the rest of the world. At 3 a.m., everyone gets into action: bathrooms are busy, training areas are readied, hot puris and chai are prepared in the battalion kitchens, and the symphony of synchronized march pasts can be heard in the distance. This energy isn't confined to the battalion area; even the homes of married officers and soldiers come alive early in the morning.

Like ours does.

The military man in the house will begin his morning ritual: shaving, ironing his clothes, preparing chai, going over the day's schedules and meetings. I am sure you will understand that if one corner of the house is filled with such activity, the rest of the house can't continue sleeping, even if there's no reason for them to be awake. Nearly half of the day's work completed within the first few hours. Though the energy levels may dip over the day, by the time the sun begins to set, the cantonment's energy revs up. The evening is filled with sports and other leisure activities. However, the most cherished part of a military person's life is brief nap after lunch.

A power nap does wonders for a fauji's system. Aside from official training schedules, this is a personal routine they have honed over time to stay energized. They don't even need a perfect atmosphere to carry out this ritual. Even during training in a classroom, they can take a quick power nap with their eyes open. Believe me, they won't even blink, but their system will shut down completely. For them, beds, mattresses and comforters are luxuries. The support of a stone or the shade of a tree will suffice if they crave sleep. One can only imagine the fatigue so deeply ingrained in their cells that they don't need any of the comforts we take for granted.

A military man can be made to work for hours, delivering at every step, regardless of time and place. He won't complain and will perform his duty without complaining one bit. But if he is granted the bliss of shutting his system, the pleasure of closing his eyes for a nap in the afternoon, he won't crave for anything else.

Surprisingly, the engine of his body does not need anything else for maintenance; just as a machine needs oil to function, a hot cup or glass of good ginger tea will do wonders. Chai is that other super fuel that works wonders for a military body. If one needs maximum output and enthusiasm from a military man, he must be fuelled with a good cup of tea. The ingredients in this cup of tea are again subject to availability, so it doesn't matter if the tea leaves belong to any brand or are local, the milk is skimmed or full cream, or whether white sugar or brown is added; the cup of tea will be judged by a military man only on its consistency after boiling. Therefore, simply create the right concoction of water, tea leaves, milk, and sugar in any ratio, and keep boiling until half of the tea evaporates. This kind of tea, or '*josh wala chai*', instils a super spirit in a fauji that nothing, no amount of work pressure, can diminish.

Try it sometime; I have tried and tested this recipe many times. It comes with the guarantee of one who has partaken of it.

13

Adventures in Baking

If '*khana banana aata hai*' (I know how to cook) works as a distinction certificate for any lady in modern India, for an army wife to be able to 'bake a cake' marks her as a meritorious lady among her peers. The reasons as to why the art of baking a cake is so popular with army wives remain unknown. My guess is that like many other traditions, we might have imbibed this from the Brits.

From her very first days as an army wife, when she struggles with transitioning from her contemporary jeans and T-shirts to more elegant attires, she is overwhelmed by another skill of army wives she has to learn: the ability to bake! In the initial days when my husband and I were struggling to set up our house, a generous dabba filled with the aroma of freshly baked goods from another home would arrive at our doorstep, neatly packed with a note stating, 'Baked it with love for you.' I watched my husband go gaga over it, devouring it and licking his fingers while endlessly complimenting the taste. I, however, saw it as more of a show-off than a modest gesture of army traditions.

At night, my naïve mind would spin various hostile reasons: 'Why did she need to send all this? *Dinner pe bula liya tha na*?' (Hadn't she invited us for dinner already?)

My overwhelmed husband would reply, 'Come on! She's just being thoughtful! Appreciate her efforts. By the way, the cake was very tasty…'

I would then shift to the other side of the bed, send her a perfunctory 'thank you' message, and quietly block her number to avoid interacting with her, even though deep down, I knew this was just insecurity and nothing else.

Gradually, I understood the warmth behind such gestures within the fauj, and with time, the desire to acquire this art grew within me. Once I started looking for avenues to learn it, I realized – and I can strongly vouch for this – that nearly every lady in the cantonment has baked or tried to bake at some point. I was fed up with the 'gyaan' on baking I got, as every time I tried, a new disaster occurred in my kitchen. I was almost losing hope and was constantly looking for a baking guru.

This experience can be equated to the fashion a few decades back when every girl wanted to learn the secret recipes of their grandmother's kitchen. The desire to master the simplest kitchen art, such as adding spices in a specific manner, worked wonders, bringing to the world hidden arts in traditional Indian kitchens, which have largely been wiped out in the era of KFC and McDonald's. Refrigerated food and fancy packaging took over health and traditions. Over time, the kitchen became less important in the house. Women who were once compared to Annapurna in our tradition were looked down upon as someone not worthy enough to go out and earn.

I noticed that in such changing times, the tradition inside the army generally stayed unaltered. I credit this to each soul breathing inside the cantonment walls. There remains this immense sense of pride in staying original, making firm decisions not based on circumstances but on the right choices at any given point in time. So, if the homemade cake is not just a cake from the market in fancy packaging, but a sign of love in an army wife's view, I had to look out for my guru and get started.

While I continued looking for a baking guru, the experiments in my kitchen went on with no success, and more and more disasters each time.

Mostly located in the boondocks of our motherland, army cantonments often feature markets where even toothpaste is referred to as Colgate, washing powder as Nirma, and noodles as Maggi. The market runs on a defined supply-and-order ratio. Choices of brands remain limited, and fake copies of original brands rule the roost. So you can get 'pissleri' water, 'Parle-F' biscuits, 'Nirmala' washing powder, and many more fancy items. Now, the struggling me, an eager army wife with full josh to assimilate into army traditions, left no stone unturned to learn the art of baking.

I found a gaudy shop in the market with a dazzling amount of fancy lights at the entrance, giving it a complete disco feel, with big cutouts of Bollywood actors and actresses holding the frame with a photo of the shop owner sitting on piles of brands, grinning at me. It definitely looked enterprising for a small place and encouraged me enough to ask for the baking ingredients, as I had used up most of them in my unsuccessful experiments back home. I realized that often, at such places, the difference between cocoa powder and coffee and that between vanilla essence and vanilla ice cream are quite difficult to explain.

I asked the shopkeeper, '*Bhaiya, maida toh hoga*?' (Bhaiya, do you have maida?)

He replied point-blank, '*Atta hai.*' (Only atta.)

I asked hopelessly, 'Brown sugar?'

He replied, '*Gur shakkar hai, madam, fresh hai, aaj hi gaon se aaya hai, doodh nahin fatega. Aur aap maida kyun khaa rahein ho, ye chakki ka atta le jaao.*' (Madam, this is jaggery sugar, and it's fresh; it just arrived from the village today. The milk won't curdle. And why are you consuming maida? Take this stone-ground whole wheat flour instead.)

To calm his enthusiasm for healthy options, I told him that I wanted to bake a cake and therefore I was looking for those particular items.

He replied enthusiastically, '*Arre! Madam, pehel bataate na! Ye wala cake le jaao.*' (Oh! Madam, you should have told me earlier! Take this cake instead.) He entered the adjoining room which had a small blue fridge, the kind of model I last saw at my grandfather's home. Then he took out a bright pink and blue whipped cream cake with a beautiful yellow lotus on top of it. I appreciated the creativity of the baker but left disheartened as now both the guru and the materials were beyond my reach.

Under such trying circumstances, what keeps a motivated soul going is their fidelity towards their goal, especially when you are married to someone who has sworn by the supreme commitment to the nation. It's natural that similar emotions flow in everyone in the family. The absence of fancy stores with the latest products will never hold an army wife back. She believes in creating wonders out of nothing.

During my search for the right guru for my baking expedition, I made some wonderful friends. By now, I was well adjusted to army life and had started getting used to its uncompetitive social life, where friendships are purely based on love, respect, and the responsibility of carrying it a long way. I realized the meaning of having true relationships, and all my frivolous, avid thoughts of acquiring, hoarding, and nurturing insecurities fizzled out.

Thereafter, as I became more attuned to the army way of life, I made friends for life. In their precious company, I learnt the importance of relationships. I also learnt that 'if a cake has to bake in an army wife's kitchen, it will bake' no matter whether you have the wherewithal or not.

I finally found my guru, who turned out to be my best friend as well. Like me, she believed in smart work and not hard work. Like a true military wife, she had the ability to use chocolate malt as cocoa powder and create her masterpieces. She taught me that a cake can be baked in a pressure cooker or kadai and the flavours can depend on the supply of fauji ration at home. Sometimes, when the supply of custard powder is abundant, the guru would alter the flavours, which in turn is budget-friendly as well. During those times, vanilla custard or caramel custard cakes are great options. If lemons are in abundance in the market, it's lemon cake; if bananas, banana cake; if suji, suji cake; if ample malai is lying in the fridge, make a malai cake. The flair for creativity in the kitchen and home is directly proportional to the salary in the military man's account. I loved the concept as much as I loved her cakes. The interesting part is that such varied experiments in the kitchen labs of a fauji wife make her such a skilled baker that she can bake anything with anything.

Therefore, now when I try to catch up with the world in big well-known cities, I can never reconcile to the fact that a piece of tart costs almost as much as the ingredients used to make a whole tray of it. But that's the allure of contemporary existence, and who doesn't love a bit of luxury, especially for a change when you step outside the cantonment gates to enjoy one of the most cherished and anticipated chapters in a military personnel's life – their leave, more popularly known as 'chhutti' for a fauji.

14

Holiday Blues

'Sandeshe aate hai
humein tadpate hai
woh chitti aati hai
toh poochhe jaate hai
ki ghar kab aaoge
likho kab aaoge'

No one can understand the utopic bliss of a fauji getting leave even though the emotions similar to the world outside the cantonment walls as well. Undoubtedly, the credit goes to all the Bollywood movies that have silver-tongued the whole narrative of the importance of getting 'chhutti' in a fauji's life.

Like in every fauji's home, in ours too, every time, without fail, the night before the day when the real 'chhutti' starts is an evening full of bittersweet emotions; sweet because finally the

'I'm officially on leave from my leave!'

leave is approved, which invariably means no early mornings, spending more time with loved ones, catching up with the outside world, and chilling out. Bitter because deep down, he knows that until he crosses the cantonment gates, it might get cancelled at the last moment. Sometimes, an emergency arises, and the leave gets cancelled even when you are right in the middle of it. Therefore, I've come to understand and accept that for a military family, 'Leave is a luxury, not a right for a true soldier!'

But then, hopefulness is another virtue found in abundance in every military soul, and the night before the real 'chhutti' starts is a moment of complete happiness in a military man's home. That night, without fail, a military man will pour a glass of scotch even if he's been battling acidity from uneven eating patterns. He will swallow antacids to settle the reflux, only to create more with the joy-juices! He will play his playlist, which only comes out from chhutti to another, as in between he neither has the time nor frame of mind to appreciate it. He will be seen in casual, easy clothing, which often surprises the wife at home, revealing her husband's surprising sense of 'contemporary men's fashion'. He will be more cheerful and savour his dinner and drinks patiently.

That's just the night-before story!

The hangover is often wiped away when domestic expectations beckon the next morning. The news of a military man getting leave travels faster than light, and with it comes plans from all quarters. From the favourite maasi who believes in only one-way communication, to the childhood friends who still wait to relive bygone times, all deliver sentimental sermons about spending time together. A major turbulence starts building up between the promises made as a husband and the responsibilities of being a son to his mother. This generally leads to a catastrophe, often resulting in a good fireworks display during the holiday!

Humans were born to be free. However, the social structure kept evolving, and over some time, the concept of 'freedom' became constrained in various ways for everyone. It was expected that to be socially accepted, one had to learn and adhere to a certain set pattern of life to be fully embraced by society. Education, customs, culture, religion, discipline, etc., evolved as ways and means to restrain the essential freedom of the human nature.

All of us yearn for a vacation because they offer that freedom as a limited-time deal. They break that pattern, set fresh priorities, put the reins of one's life in their hands, and shatter the glass ceiling that cages the free soul – if only momentarily! But who cares if someone working 24/7 in the hinterlands gets to taste such freedom even for a brief moment?

Soon, the packing begins; civilian clothes, buried inside the fauji trunks, finally see the light and get transferred to jazzy suitcases and bags. Chiffon saris and pearls are stowed away, and jeans, T-shirts, and dresses are pulled out. After all, vacations are the only time for a military family to catch up with the jazzy flares of life, fashion, and food seen in movies and Instagram reels.

Cut To…

I find myself standing with my family at the main atrium of the most talked-about mall in Delhi, surrounded by stores brimming with the latest fashion, food, coffee, makeup, décor, shoes, jewellery, and more. The city looks nothing like I left it a few years ago; every soul moving around looks like a model on a ramp, displaying trendy fashion with coordinated shoes, makeup, and the latest hair colours. The brightly lit ambience and loud music make it feel like one has stepped into a metaverse. My reflection in the large mirrors in the stores reminds me that I am probably the only old-fashioned, primitive individual around here. I look like yesterday's leftover.

The clothes I wore had been bought during the previous season's summer sale, when the military man got his last leave. Now, with the whole world moving in high-waisted loose jeans, I found myself wandering around in boot cuts or last season's jeggings. But because confidence and grace cannot be bought – and are abundant within the cantonment walls – our military family marched around confidently, exploring the world, even if we mentally didn't belong there anymore.

It's intriguing to see twenty varieties of coffee with twenty more flavours to add on; a simple burger is no longer just a bun and patty, but so much more. Cakes and biscuits come in flour options that cater to everyone from diabetes to those with allergies. Being used to a simpler, less flamboyant lifestyle, it was unfathomable. I have nothing against the gimmicks of the contemporary market, but I don't understand why, when somebody needs just a cup of coffee and two cookies, the options on offer are enough to drive you batty.

Why must one read an entire coffee encyclopaedia? Oh, sorry! Not even read – first, you have to scan those QR codes, and if you have a high-tech phone and your data pack is working, you will then start another list of choices: sugar, flavour, flour, etc. After all this mental effort, you end up paying for all the choices you've made yourself. And let me tell you, the paying part is also not that simple – PayTm, Google Pay, credit card, debit card, gift card.

Before long we realized that half of my military man's monthly salary was spent exploring the ground and first floor of the mall. The man who could carry 10 kg and complete a 10 km route in 25 minutes suddenly succumbed to exhaustion and started searching for the exit doors to escape this hall of financial ruin.

The city outside never sleeps – it's as exciting in the day as at night! Offering so much visual delight to outsiders like a military family. The mere drive through the underpass with world-class lighting, the air-conditioned metro trains and their speed, the well-lit humongous buildings, LED screens with advertisements, traffic lights, well-lit roads with the latest cars zooming by feels nothing less than an adventurous ride at Disney World.

The mornings of a chhutti day for a military man begin quite normally, especially when he has visited his parents, as no matter what ranks they keep achieving or how many stars shine on their shoulder, it's all about loving your parents. Though the first few days remain special, with parathas with extra makhan in the morning to chicken cooked in the traditional family way, TV volumes are kept low while the military man sleeps like a log in the other room. He will be pampered like a soldier who has come home after fighting a war.

However, this pampering doesn't last long. The role reversal, from being an '*aakhon ka taara*' (apple of the eye) to becoming '*budhape ki laathi*' (old age's support), happens in a snap, followed by a massive attack of expectations, with bombardments of work from all sides. At the home station, the morning responsibility for a military man invariably starts as a driver, visiting the sabzi mandi to buy fresh veggies for his mother, who wants to feed him dishes that remind him of '*bachpan ke din*' (childhood days). He then proceeds to drop his wife at the salon, as she too has returned to civilization after a long time. Further, the transformation between driver and son continues, as he drives from one specialist to another for his parents' health check-ups, unsure of when he will get leave again.

Amidst all these shenanigans, the only soul who feels on vacation and is making the best out of the military man's leave is his child who gets an opportunity to interact with new faces and gets indulged by both sides of the family, something which children miss in their daily life within cantonment walls. The child's overexcitement, screaming, and rushing up and down the stairs go mostly unnoticed by the two opposing teams of grandparents and who put their best foot forward to try and outdo each other in loving their grandchild.

Children get an opportunity to explore different local places, museums, and monuments while their parents become their chauffeur. Every evening, the child ends the day with some crazy junk food which is otherwise prohibited and is a punishable offence under motherly reign within the cantonment.

Military families remain quite restricted within their cantonment boundaries, so the socialization mostly happens at wedding functions and at local grocery shops. And these two options remain quite limited and similar every year as there are only a limited number of families living in a military station. The weddings that military families attend, and shopping in cantonments, bear no comparison to the extravagant, large, and beautiful functions organized in civilian life. The celebrations in civilian life start a month before the D-day and end with the last Instagram post.

So, this too becomes an integral part of the military family's itinerary while on leave. They get to be part of at least one such event in their extended family. The hunt for the wedding card begins as soon as leave is granted, and the choice of which one to attend depends on the duration of the leave granted. For the wife of a soldier, this is the only time she too can get dolled up and get a good blow-dry and step into the world she only sees in advertisements.

The army wife becomes excited – finally, she too will get an opportunity to dress up, just like the influencers on social media. Thus, the bag she carried to attend the wedding and other family functions is the most colourful one and is filled with jewels, makeup, and best saris. Though she tries to keep up with the latest fashion, the sad part is she has only memories of what is in fashion in civilian life, but being absorbed in family duties, she doesn't even realize when one fashion goes and the other comes. She can only hope that in the circularity of fashion, she finds herself in vogue.

The wedding and family functions are spheres where a

military family is most vulnerable, as they have no control over the situation. From the time of leave, travel plans, mode of travel, and cash in hand, everything is decided by someone else's system. They don't easily fit in, but they do try their best to remain incognito. They fail at this, but no one can spot their misery behind the dazzling uniform they are accustomed to wearing all the time.

Despite trying their best to be in civilian attire, a soldier and his family get noticed by all. The wife, who doesn't carry the latest handbags and shoes, is looked down on by other womenfolk. And when they ask, 'Where did you get it from?' the wives generally reply, with some pride, 'From the cantonment store.' However, this is enough to make them realize how different they are from the crowd. The poor soldier doesn't get noticed at all, aside from the fauji moustache, haircut, and too well-behaved etiquettes. The money he spends on himself becomes a matter of concern as he tries to save enough to buy his son a bicycle for his fifth birthday or that beautiful suit his wife was eyeing in the big mall. He wonders if it's even worth it.

But the smile remains intact on his face. With a camera in hand, he will click photographs at the wedding – photos that mostly go unused, as when his wife sees them later, she finds that her fauji has captured the best angles of his family and children, but not the couple tying the knot.

The once-a-year chhutti further complicates matters with frantic calls from relatives wanting to meet the bahu, bachhe, and the military man. For instance, on the fifteenth day of our precious chhutti, we decided to visit Pappi Mausi, who probably last saw the military man in a nikkar and baniyan, playing with the plastic gun she gifted him on Diwali. While sipping masala chai, quite akin to Pappi Mausi's spicy personality, we go through old albums, reliving bygone days with flavoursome gupshup.

Though like a typical Indian family, a military family, too enjoys all the khatirdari and attention, it soon starts to nag. Just explaining your posting location feels like reciting a geography textbook. The ever-inquisitive mausi asks, '*Kahan posted hai tu aaj kal?*' (Where are you posted these days?) Virtually, a big book of geography opens before us, and the military man starts explaining.

Military Man: '*Lal Garh mein Maasi.*' (Maasi, it is in Lal Garh.)

Maasi: '*Hain! Woh kahan hai?*' (Where is that?)

Military Man: '*Hanumangarh ke paas.*' (Near Hanumangarh.)

Maasi: '*Ab woh kahan hai?*' (Now where is this place?)

Military Man: '*Ganganagar ke paas.*' (Near Ganganagar.)

Maasi: '*Yamuna Nagar? Punjab mein hai tu?*' (Yamuna Nagar? Are you in Punjab?)

Military Man: '*Nahin, Ganganagar jo Abohar ke paas hai. Woh Bathinda ke paas hai, Bathinda Hisar ke paas hai, Hisar Rohtak ke paas hai, Rohtak Delhi ke paas hai.*' (No, Ganganagar, which is near Abohar, which is close to Bathinda. Bathinda is near Hisar, Hisar is near Rohtak, and Rohtak is near Delhi.)

Maasi: '*Matlab tu Delhi ke paas hi hai? Dekha phir bhi nahin aata mujhse milne.*' (So, you're close to Delhi? See, even then you don't come to meet me.)

The military man, looking at maasi, contemplates the saying, 'Silence is the best defence,' and finally leaves, accepting the blame for neglecting personal relations for work.

By the twenty-fifth day of the military man's precious chhutti, he feels:

1. Bankrupt from trying to keep up with the civilian resto-pub-mall culture.
2. Emotionally drained from being '*Maa-Baap ka sahaara*'.
3. Fatigued by the virtue of '*rishtey nibhao*'.

The feeling is nothing less than being at war, sapped to the core. No matter which side you're defending, you long to return home. In our case, after all the aspirations to catch up with the civilian world, we now earnestly long to get back within the cantonment gates, where we once again embrace the abstinence of a Spartan life, with the most prized aspect being the character chiselled by living a life of utmost discipline and integrity.

However, despite all these weighty attributes, '*Dil to bachha hai ji, aur thodi chhutti sab ke liye achhi hai ji!*' (The heart is still a child, and a little break is good for everyone.)

And with all this in our hearts, we return to the military way of life, nurturing the sweet hope of getting chhutti again and experiencing its bittersweet charm all over again.

15

'Guard the Igloo': Bas Yun Hi!

'*Bas yun hi*' or 'Just like that,' as we say in English, is a very rare expression in a setup like the military, where almost everything in its ecosystem is meticulously planned.

Aside from the extensive military planning of our nation, where every twist and turn of roads, bridges, curves, and depths of jungles and hills is marked and strategized for the nation's absolute security, even seemingly insignificant fences, trees, or piles of stones around a military station are meticulously mapped out. If you observe closely, the Neem, Amaltas, or Gulmohar trees along the cantonment roads are painted in uniform stripes of chuna and geru, standing in absolute alignment, resonating with the spirit of militarism.

In such a scenario, where's the room for 'bas yun hi' kind of whimsy?

I too thought so, until the Pandora's Box of 'bas yun hi' in the fauj knocked me down. Babina is a suburb encompassing the famous town of Jhansi, widely known as the land of Rani Lakshmi Bai. Babina, a needle in a haystack on contemporary Indian geographical maps, is considered the Manhattan of the Indian Armed Forces maps. It is an abbreviated form of 'British Army Base in Northern Asia,' and perhaps that's why, even after the British Raj, it remained a major army base like many others established during colonial times.

Amusingly, aside from this historical significance, there is nothing fancy about the place. As luck would have it, we received our first major posting here after the wedding. And like all the other wonderful things I've learned as an army wife, I have also mastered the art of tuning my mind so that the present problem seems smaller than the past ones. This attitude makes any arising issue appear easier to handle.

The army teaches us to be positive in every scenario and fearless about the ambiguities of military life, or life as a whole. Therefore, the fact remains that, even if we are posted in the middle of nowhere with no jazzy or snazzy things around, we still believe in sailing through it without complaints. With that thought in my mind and heart, I unpacked on an extremely humid and hot summer afternoon in Babina, or 'Babs' as we affectionately call it, where Surya Devta generously provided free sauna baths to everyone and shone with abundant warmth on all mortal souls.

In moments like these, as you unpack and prepare to set up a barren house that may have stood on that land for many years, with countless families creating bittersweet memories, you observe it deeply. You plan the interiors, mentally fit your furniture, and visualize how the corners will look once the house is set up. After much trial and error, you achieve setting everything in place, making it your own. On one of the pleasant evenings, after everything was done and the house was ready to military standards, it was time to enjoy the fruits of our hard work. My beloved military man and I enjoyed a cup of tea in the garden in fine porcelain, while he, busy with his files and calls, tried to adjust to his new course of work and responsibilities.

Then I heard him give orders to send 'four men to guard the Igloo'. I heard it again the next day and realized that every day a few men were sent to guard the Igloo, or 'Igloo ki guard' as it was referred to. The idea of guarding an Igloo in the extremely warm place of Babina made no sense to me. My curiosity led me to the military man, and I inquired about it while sitting in the garden during teatime, which soon turned into cold coffee time due to the extreme warmth.

'I heard you're setting a guard for an Igloo. Where is this Igloo when the ice is melting in the freezer?' I asked.

With gleaming eyes, the military man replied calmly, 'It's not that ice Igloo, but rather an Igloo-shaped structure that requires guarding.'

Astonished, I asked further, 'What is so special about it?'

Amazed by my question, the military man replied, 'Nothing!'

I later learned that the structure was created as part of a plan, and something was strategized around it. However, the plan was eventually scrapped, and nothing major ever happened there. Surprisingly, the Igloo structure remained in perpetuity, and to protect this 'coveted' building, guards were routinely allocated.

So, 'bas yun hi!' Every night, four to five people guarded the desolate structure of 'the Igloo' vigilantly and were referred to as the much sought-after 'Igloo ki guard'. That was my introduction to the 'yun hi' splinter group of the fauj.

Over the years, I encountered many such occasions where the reasons for the existence of some things were obscure and made no sense. What made it hilarious was the diligent adherence to these rituals, even when the rationale was unspecified.

For instance, whenever the fauji phone rang at home and the call was from a senior officer, he would ensure that the distress signal was immediately passed. Within a flash, I, now an adept military wife, would pick up the kids, switch off the TV (even during crucial moments of a favourite show, like discovering why Kattappa killed Bahubali), and shut the door. The room would transform from a relaxed, luxurious space with kids playing, Netflix at high volume, and beer and wine flowing, into a quiet, military-like operation room. The sound from the other side would be inaudible, with the only word repeated in intervals being a crisp 'Sir!' This would be followed by another 'Sir' and a series of 'Sir's,' culminating in a 'Jai Hind Sir,' signalling that the curfew had been lifted, and normalcy could resume: the children could play again, the maid could use the grinder, and Netflix could continue.

As a wife, I often wondered why such theatrical arrangements were made at home, why the military man stood the whole time he spoke to his senior, who couldn't even see him, through the archaic fauji phones. But then, 'Bas yun hi!'

I could never understand why the time after midday is referred to in hours rather than a more colloquial manner. For instance, why is 5 p.m. not 5 p.m. but 1700 hours, and 1 p.m. is 1300 hours, etc., in the military? Imagine the plight of someone with a non-mathematical background like me, who had to do the whole calculation and counting just to know the time!

But then, 'Bas yun hi!'

What further amazes me is when the most popular and widely known fauji rations arrive at a military home, the expiry dates present another challenge. For instance, sometimes we receive a bulk delivery of dry rations for 2-3 months, which might include five bottles of pineapple fruit jam, three packets of choco malt, and five dabbas of cheese. The challenge is that everything expires within a month! The rationale for it falls under the all-encompassing rubric of 'bas yun hi'.

In such scenarios, where the usual approach would be to either distribute it to the housemaid or discard it, a typical military wife, who embraces challenges and values saving every penny of the precious salary, comes up with various plans to make effective use of it. From hot cheese parathas to chilled cheese salads and from pineapple jelly to choco malt laddoos, everything will be subjected to my culinary trials.

Although I could never fully understand this amusing axiom of military life being followed so rigidly, and my 'aware' and 'wise' self often tried to find reasons, I concluded that adventure is found in the unknown. I have always believed, '*Jo samajh aa jaye, woh zindagi bhi kya zindagi hai*!' (What is life worth if you understand it all!)

16

The Black Boxes

The first time I heard this term was during one bright summer vacation in the 1990s, when holidays meant spending days reading comics, playing outdoors endlessly, and not to forget films on the VCR! The whole family would plan which movies to watch, and videocassettes would be rented or borrowed from video parlours and then returned after watching for a nominal price. Though I don't remember exactly which movie it was, I vaguely recall that during one of the very dramatic scenes, when the plane crashed and all the top secrets on board were destroyed, the genius protagonist, with exceptional aptitude, Bond-like charisma, and Rambo-like physique, alluded to 'The Black Box' to unravel the suspense and solve the mysteries ahead. Besides being thoroughly entertained, my young mind grasped the importance of the black box in the whole movie. The term 'The Black Box' was etched into the memory card of my mind for a long time, generating the same curiosity it did when I first heard it. For a long time, the term 'The Black Box' always conjured up something highly confidential, integral, and mysterious. Little did I know that the whole narrative of the discreet black boxes etched in my memory would be redefined into something much more amusingly contrasting yet similar.

The journey of collecting the all-important black boxes, more popularly known as 'baksas', starts in a military man's life as soon as he gets married and shifts from the bachelor barracks to the married quarters. Initially, the purpose of the black box remains the same: storage. The contents are typically minimal: two pairs of civil formal clothes, two pairs of jeans, a few uniforms, some books, a few albums from the academy days, and one or two keepsakes bought from the local markets in anticipation that they might come in handy when we set up our home. Surprisingly, the number of 'baksas' is also a sign of prosperity in the Indian Army, as with every posting, the number increases. While a young captain might possess one or two, by the time he retires, the number may have swelled to forty or fifty. The faded layers of paint on the boxes reflect the various ranks the officer has held. In one corner, the rank of captain might still be visible, while other ranks, such as major or colonel, are also obvious. Thus, these coveted black boxes tell the story of an officer's life in every way.

When we started our journey, our whole house fit into just two baksas, properly sealed with my husband's name and rank clearly marked on them. I never thought that six pairs of Borasil glasses, four pairs of glass bowls, a few coffee mugs, a pressure cooker, a kadhai, and a few more kitchen gadgets would require such careful packaging. It almost felt like smuggling when we had to cover each item in its original packaging and then wrap it multiple times in different layers, starting with the newspapers saved from last year, then progressing to the sturdy brown cardboard, then the multipurpose green hessian cloth, and finally completing the process with the fragments of old, torn dupattas and bed sheets.

All of this was packed inside the black baksa and sealed, ready for the next location. With these layers, the knowledge of what lies beneath is completely forgotten. It's manageable when the baksas are in the single digits, but as the military man's rank increases and the number of postings adds up, it becomes a veritable cave of wonders – though only a resourceful army wife would know its secrets!

Incidentally, for a fauji, handling the baksas during transfers is one thing; managing them in a 2-BHK house for the next 2.5 years is another. After the initial unpacking and setup, the next herculean task is storing the wrappers for the next move, besides the original paper or cardboard wraps, which can still be layered and put under the heavy mattresses or thrown into the abyss of unused lofts in every government house. One cannot discard them, because in two years when the next location is announced, they will be required again, so they must be kept and preserved until then.

When God closes one door, He opens another. While I was struggling with the dilemma of managing my 100 baksas spread all around the house, we received an invitation from one of the senior officers as a welcome gesture, a part of the military protocol to welcome the newly arrived couple to the station.

It was during that dinner that the old saying in the army, 'In the fauj, you learn from your seniors,' came true. I was preoccupied with the thought of making my new abode comfortable, and simultaneously admiring the aesthetics of the host. With a lot of hesitation and a bit of courage after gulping down two glasses of red wine, I finally threw the question that had been troubling me for a while: 'What do you do with the black boxes, Mrs Sharma? Where do you store them?'

The smirk on Mrs Sharma's face almost confirmed that certain skills can only be refined with time. Silently, I followed her as she walked with confidence straight to her bedroom to show me her secrets. The MES bed stood in the centre, neatly clad with block-printed bedsheets and bed covers, lamps and plants accentuating the warmth of the room. Two low seats on either corners of the room with bookshelves looked just perfect, until Mrs Sharma removed the beautiful throws that I had been admiring. To my astonishment, the boxes, the black 'baksas', were under the beautiful throws, properly cushioned and creatively used as low seating. Mrs Sharma further revealed that not just seating, but the TV stand, study table, and even the mandir of the house were placed atop the black boxes. All this while I was struggling to manage them, and suddenly, with all this creativity around, it turned out they could be so useful. I could never have imagined them being used in such varied ways. Thrilled with Mrs Sharma's innovations, I left the party, gave her a sisterly hug, and thanked her for the invitation which lifted my inexperienced military wife burdens and brought me a step closer to becoming one of the many multitalented army wives known for their simple, effortless, ingenious persona.

A few days later, my house was ready just the way I wanted it: light curtains, floral upholsteries, a few lamps, and fresh plants. And yes! The black boxes were all perfectly placed – in their 'right places'. In my home, such 'right places' are the little mysteries of an army household, where we camouflage the smudged and create our silver linings. After all, '*Ye bhi ek art hai.*' (This too is an art.)

17

Separation Pangs: Mere Piya Gaye Rangoon

मेरे पिया
ओ मेरे पिया गए रंगून
किया है वहाँ से टेलीफून
तुम्हारी याद सताती है
तुम्हारी याद सताती है
जिया में आग लगाती है

The sentiments of this song, sung by Shamshad Begum in 1949 remain relevant to many army wives today, as separation is a reality of military life. Although a military man stays away from his family from the day he is commissioned into this coveted service to the nation and serves wherever duty demands, the intensity of separation increases manifold, especially when the soldier is married, has children, or leaves his pregnant wife behind to handle the house, school, and relations, and most importantly, the emotional upheavals that arise from these long separations in one's mind and heart.

In today's contemporary world, where science and technology have evolved to such an extent that a simple touch of a button connects you to the whole world, things have become so easy and accessible that all this cybernetics is to quite an extent child's play. Therefore, as we breathe in such a modern era, it becomes even more difficult for the rest of the world to understand what brews inside the low-tech homes of the man guarding this highly evolved, space-aged country. Besides the big sacrifices like family separation, undefined working hours without extra pay, isolated tours of duty, and of course, putting his life at stake, he also makes a lot of minor yet imperative sacrifices, with limited internet availability due to security concerns being one of them.

In a military home, the pain and struggle to at least stay telephonically connected can be equated to the depiction of a love story in Shamshad Begum's famous song from 1949, with which I begin this essay. Still, most of the time, phone calls do not go through due to poor connectivity, and video calls are barred due to security concerns. Often, the child forgets what the father looked like and cries his heart out when he sees the tanned, stony-faced individual trying to hold him once he returns from duty. The housemaid might even ask the wife about the stranger roaming in the house like mine did one day:

'*Memsahib, yeh kaun sahib hai? Aapke bhai hain kya?*' (Madam, who is this gentleman? Is he your brother?)

These are just a few struggles arising from these long, silent separations. Nevertheless, life goes on in the army, and that too with the utmost graciousness. That's the beauty of being inside the cantonment walls.

For some, naturally, the 'separation' period becomes a long, sad, and gloomy stretch of time, where even a day feels like a year and every responsibility a burden. It's difficult when you don't have that partner who vowed to stay with you through thick and thin during the never-ending pheras in shaadi, and you curse being left alone to deal with everything all by yourself.

I also feel that no words can ever capture the void you feel when you stand alone for things, but I also believe that a true army wife, with the right josh in her (which she passively acquires living with her military man), would convert this time into a period of self-growth, rejoicing in it with her tribe of other army wives. Amusingly, for a true army wife, this is also a time to have fun with her gang!

So, during one such long separation when I was staying back in the cantonment alone, with *main aur meri tanhai*, and the tanhai part was getting a little too much and boring, a brainwave struck me: to have a five o'clock tea with my lady friends. Without much ado, I rang everyone, and they all agreed. Bingo! An evening was planned.

The amusing part of this evening was that, on the surface, it looked like just a time to catch up with friends over Earl Grey's and coffee. However, at a deeper level, this was the ultimate time for the host to flaunt the best gourmet spread she had learned, showcase her interior skills by putting the right flowers in the right vases, and spread the right tablecloths with the most exclusive designs. This becomes her ShowTime of military hospitality, and for some unexplainable reason, army wives, and only army wives, would understand how it feels at such a moment: what she has gathered through her numerous shopping sprees, bought at the most competitive rates, haggled her lungs out for, and saved that extra dosh to get the matching dollies with the flowers just to add that typical military wife vintage art to do up the space with the utmost grace and style.

Coming back to the five o'clock tea, this was the time to manifest all my innovations, creating an oomph moment for everyone, and consequently, the same moment would also put me out there as an accomplished sarv-gun-sampan army wife! An image to strive for!

Besides the choices of teas, cake, and sandwiches, it's in vogue nowadays to add some sort of activity or game to your parties. It not only breaks the monotony but also serves as a great icebreaker and works to stimulate the energy. Such choices remain popular, especially if the invitees are women who love to 'sniff' the food and 'talk' about health at all times. With games, they get to move, stir, and be in action, rather than being restricted to the corner of a sofa and behaving ladylike all the time.

So, I thought of going ahead with this popular choice. Considering that, I racked my brain and scanned all possible party games on the internet, which only left me more confused and wasted my precious hours just before the party. In vain, while still thinking about the game choices as I was setting the tea table, out of nowhere I thought of croquet! This fit perfectly with my so-called 'English-Tea evening' setup! Without delay, the croquet set was organized, and the holes in the lawns were dug to fix the wickets.

In army parties, when the ladies come, the children are complementary. So, I had to plan to keep them busy as well. However, children being children, no matter what I plan, they will end up playing their own way. So, I didn't plan anything concrete but kept the safest kids' games played in the army, which I'm sure even the oldest military kid alive in the world would have played as a child at mess parties: passing the parcel, statue dance, and musical chairs. I thought of making the eldest kids responsible for conducting it, as I would be busy with their mothers. Just to be on the safe side, I kept an ample supply of juices and chips so that they could enjoy their own little party.

Everything glowed perfectly in the evening sun: the lush green lawns, which I watered daily; the off-white drapes in the gazebo, which had got a few stain marks in the last shift, but I dyed them back; the vintage chairs with floral upholstery, which I bought at second-hand rates from a retiring officer's wife; the spread of snacks, all made at home; the tea cakes, which I recently learned to make from a senior lady in the army; and the choices of tea in the fine porcelain, which I bought online during the Diwali sale. Finally, the croquet set, which I borrowed from the army mess for the evening, and of course, the chips and juices from the canteen for the children. It all turned out so beautifully, just the way I wanted it. At last, when my guests arrived with their kids, the whole space was filled with so much happiness and warmth.

After the initial mandatory compliments on the house and food, the ladies had to gossip to digest whatever little they had eaten. Thus, a chain reaction started from one to the other until we had discussed almost everyone within the cantonment. The non-stop banter and laughs we had at every missed stroke of the mallet were priceless! For God's sake! Who knew how to play croquet? Though it started the original way, it then converted to hockey, then cricket, and a little bit of golf was also tried. It hardly mattered whether we played it right or not; in the pictures, we looked perfect with every stroke, and that's what matters for a lady at the end of any party; good photos must be clicked.

Finally, sapped of energy, we all sat on the lawn, and the emotional half of us miserably remembered our better halves, the happiness they bring to the home, and how the children miss them every time they go to bed. But then I realized that before it all starts getting too emotional and the mood changes, I should switch gears. So, I started making them count the benefits of husbands being away: no five o'clock alarm, no breakfast to prepare, no one to share the remote with – and we all laughed again endlessly.

They were keeping their shoulders to the wheel at some desolate location far from all of us, with the faith in their hearts that the women behind were holding the fort for their families and staying happy, just as we were at that moment, laughing with glittering joy in our eyes.

Feeling the moment, I thought of the famous lines I read somewhere: '*Life is a matter of choices, and the choice you make makes you.*' An army wife has all the reasons to limit herself and blame it on the baggage, or the 'black boxes' I have mentioned if you will, of the conditions that come with her husband's profession. She, however, unapologetically paints her own horizon every time with the limited colours she has in hand.

Separations, distance, and many such gaps in relationships can lead to extreme loneliness and negativity. Invariably, in the army, one has to go through such times constantly, and therefore a lot rests on the shoulders of the lady left back at home. It matters what choices she makes and how she keeps the mood of the family when she has a million reasons to break down. Her happiness in life strengthens the military man's faith in the system, knowing that it is taking care of his family when he is not around for them. It is not just the perks and privileges any system provides, but what holds us together is the ritual and traditions we follow: a tradition of bumping into each other's lives when feeling alone, a ritual of visiting each other's houses during festivals, the spirit of taking care of your neighbour's children when their mother is out for work, a tradition of friendship so thick and deep that time and distance cannot make any difference. The wives of military men come together and form their own system, strong enough to keep all the cracks concealed and make their micro world a happy place to live.

It is said that you can't choose your neighbours. Well, in the army, you can!

18

Wah! Womaniya!

The fauj is generally portrayed through cinema and news as being all about masculinity, the 'man thing'. It's about the tough life they live, their training, their skills, and so on. Although the importance of army wives and their contributions is captured, they are usually included in the story to provide emotional embellishments. For example, whenever a soldier is leaving for war, a scene of a crying bride is almost mandatory. This reminds me of Nirupa Roy, who, whenever she appeared on screen, brought an emotional depth to Amitabh's movies, leaving the audience teary and filled with motherly love. This kind of emotional portrayal generally sells and is maintained in most fauji movies.

There's a lot to the story of women in the army, and I may not be able to mention them all. Women play a pivotal role in running the organization and are the soft power of the system. It's not just the officers' wives who are part of this; a large number of soldiers' wives also contribute significantly. AWWA, or the Army Wives' Welfare Association, is the umbrella organization under which all the wives, children, and dependents of army officers and soldiers fall. It's a non-profit NGO with the sole aim of empowering every woman in the Indian Army, coming from varied backgrounds, through various schemes and programmes run systematically.

This may sound a bit too serious compared to the lighter tales I've shared so far. Before you start comparing army wives to the dramatic portrayal of Nirupa Roy, let me share the lighter moments, the laughs, and the memories we create while working diligently towards our mission of happiness and empowerment for all army wives under AWWA.

There is a system in the army wherein every month and sometimes even more frequently, all the ladies, including officers' and soldiers' wives, meet to interact and bond. This bond amongst the ladies of the army is crucial, especially during crises when circumstances may require us to support each other. Besides this prime aim, we also attend these meetings to foster deep connections with each other. Here, even senior army wives guide the newcomers about the army way of life, which, being different from their previous life, brings significant change for an individual. Such meets also cover various schemes to enhance skills, educational projects where women can complete their education or pursue a course, children's educational programmes, and many other essential and relevant topics. All of this is carried out in a highly systematic manner with clear guidelines.

Though these meetings generally follow a formal plan, but elements of fun and frolic through games and competitions are also included. These additions often break the ice between wives of different ranks and help them connect better. Above all, I feel women like to be treated as women, and once that is done, they connect automatically. Their likes and dislikes, their pain, and their conversations bring them together faster than anything else in this world.

One such meeting was organized about 25 km away from our settlement in an adjoining cantonment, where a senior official from Delhi was coming to introduce us to various AWWA-related features. We along with a group of fifty ladies, including officers' and jawans' wives, were detailed to attend it. Such meetings are nothing like the conferences or orientation programmes held in civilian setups, where the venue is typically a five-star hotel with air-conditioned conference halls, free tea and coffee with snacks, attendees in formal suits with the latest branded laptops, and the programme ends with a lavish lunch and goodie bags. On the contrary, this was a meet in the Indian Army setup, so the sanctity of the event had to be maintained.

Therefore, first and foremost, we had to dress according to our perpetual dress code: a sari! And before your imagination starts comparing us to glamorous Karan Johar heroines with low-tied saris, scanty blouses, and sensuous makeup, holding books and pens for class, let me clarify that the saris worn by army wives are very much like a 'sari' in the purest sense, reflecting how a national dress should be. We adhere to a proper draping style and believe in staying elegantly classic, cutting out all the fashion flares. Likewise, we select our six yards of grace and dignity and start planning our day before heading out to the meeting.

Here I need to bring the context of a basic army household back into the story, where the responsibility for the entire household lies with the lady. If she is leaving for any work, she must arrange everything from her husband's meals to the pet's, as she literally cannot leave anything disorganized. It has nothing to do with the 'responsibility ka bojh' but rather the principle that, for the husbands, their duty to the nation comes first. Due to the intensity of their work, they are not significantly available for the 'sharing of responsibility'. Thus, a true military wife assumes the role of the 'man' in the house. She chooses this life and adopts this formula to run her house smoothly.

For soldiers' wives, home management takes an extra leap; she generally handles cleaning, cooking, and grocery shopping all on her own, without any sign of regret. Then when an official engagement arises, it requires extra planning. An army wife typically plans so well that everything from home to the engagement falls into place. The first step is the 5 o'clock alarm. Everything in the army is time-bound, and a lot of emphasis is placed on time management. All events, whether for officers, soldiers, or ladies, follow a specific timeline. (Even birthday parties for kids start precisely on time; if the invite says 6 p.m. for cake cutting, the cake will be cut at exactly 6 p.m., no matter what.)

Such events usually occur in the morning hours. The lady of the house wakes up two hours before the event, completes all her household responsibilities, dons her sari with a bindi and comfortable sandals, and heads out with full military spirit to attend, learn, and sometimes simply enjoy with her friends. In normal circumstances, a 25-km journey in the scorching summer heat, dressed in a sari, to attend a lecture, might seem excessive. However, for an army wife with a motivated attitude instilled by the spirited environment we live in, it feels like a minor task. It's an opportunity to do something beyond the mundane, to discuss topics beyond household issues, make bonds, laugh, and simply enjoy.

In the army, maintaining hierarchy and following orders is a key aspect, primarily for officers and men. Among the ladies, hierarchy is maintained to some extent but is generally more fluid. Relationships can range from formal to friendly and casual, depending on their familiarity. However, a thin line of military custom always exists to maintain order and discipline.

Returning to the story, on one of these days, we had to attend the lecture. We all gathered in a military bus assigned to take us to the venue. I chose not to travel in my own vehicle to be with everyone, as it is more enjoyable. All the women were from my battalion, whom I've known for over a decade. Travelling together is always more fun than being alone in a separate vehicle with a stony-faced military driver and the hum of the air conditioner.

I made the wise choice of taking the bus. As I adjusted the pallu of my crisp ironed khadi cotton sari to avoid spoiling it, a lance naik's wife, Rupa, whom I've known since I joined the battalion as a married woman, joked in her typical Haryanvi tone, '*Namaste memsahib, aap bade achhe lag rahe ho.*'

I replied in the same tone, to keep the mood light, '*Rupa, aap bhi bade achhe lag rahe ho in sari*' (Rupa, you also look very nice in this saree) and smiled. She knew I was teasing her, as Haryanvi wives are usually not fond of saris and are used to wearing suits.

Rupa replied, '*Memsahibji, subha se lagi hui hu isse pehnne main. Aaj toj breakfast main bhi parathe nahin, roti banayi thi, time nahin tha. Memsahibji, kal maine Bhagat Singh ki picture dekhi TV main, aur aaj sabhi ko sari aur iss bus main dekh ke aisa lag raha hai jaise hum Gandhiji ke lecture sunne ke liye jaa rahe hain.*' (Madam, I've been struggling with wearing this sari since morning. I didn't even make parathas for breakfast today, just roti, as there was no time. Madam, yesterday I watched a film on Bhagat Singh on TV, and today, seeing all of us in saris and this bus, it feels like we are going to listen to a lecture by Gandhiji.)

And I actually felt the uniformity of our attire! She was right! We all dressed alike in simple, decent cotton saris, reminiscent of the revolutionary women of the pre-independence era, travelling in groups to attend anti-British lectures. Then, as the driver bhaiya started the engine, it roared and stopped faintly.

Seeing this, his wife from the back seat, who was also joining us for the lecture, shouted in her Bihari tone, '*Mohan ke papa, ye bus kyun nahin start kar rahe ho? Aap jaan ke nahin kar rahe honge. Aaj main lecture ke liye jaa rahi hoon. Lag raha hai hum angrezo ke zamane ki bus main jaa rahe hain, hai na madamji!*' (Mohan's father, why isn't this bus starting? You must be doing it deliberately. I am going to the lecture today. It feels like we are travelling in a bus from the British era, doesn't it, madam?)

Everyone laughed, and I thought that such humour in an otherwise serious event made the journey less monotonous. As soon as the engine roared and we were on our way, the journey began to feel less tedious. We reached the venue on time, and the day went well. Many ladies gathered, sharing experiences, laughing, and chatting over tea and snacks. Such events always end on a lighter note.

Although I began with a serious tone, these lighter moments bring a smile to my face even today. Such journeys and days have been among the most memorable.

19

The Ichhadhari Army Wife

Before you start imagining, '*Nahin hum dasti nahin*' – no, we do not bite. *Haan Rajasthan ke deserts mai bahut posting kaati hai, aur apne gharon ke garden main bahut baar saapo ko tahalte bhi dekha hai, aur itna dekha hai ki shayad yahan vardaan humein unn se hi mila hai – ichhadhari hai but without zehar*! (Yes, we have had many postings in the deserts of Rajasthan and have seen snakes in our gardens many times, so much so that perhaps our blessing comes from them – ichhadhari but without poison!)

Sometimes, when I sit in peace, alone with a cup of hot coffee, and wonder about how my days are spent in the army as a wife, I often relate it to the adventurous storybooks I read as a child. How the princess enters the 'la shear land' through a tree hollow and how with every stroke of the hour, the colour of her dresses changes, how with just a soft touch of a flower, the whole jungle glows, and how with just one command, the fairy godmother turns the colour of the whole place into something beautiful and more exciting.

I strongly feel we army wives live a similar life. The facets of being an army wife are so bewildering and magical that they leave an enchanting trail behind.

Mostly, an army wife who has been with her military man long enough and has experience of at least five to six postings together would relate to how important it is to always be alert with our husbands and their last-minute revelations of crucial matters. '*Aree yaar! Aaj to sabhi ko ghar bulana hi padega*!' (Oh no! Today we must invite everyone home!). Or '*Mera bhai, mera coursemate yahan se gujar raha tha to dinner pe bula liya*!' (My brother, my coursemate, was passing through here, so I invited him for dinner!). Or '*Aree yaar! Aaj to dining-in party hai*!' (Oh no! Today is a dining-in party!). These keep dropping in abruptly like an unguided missile from nowhere on the lady of the house, and she is undoubtedly expected to manage it all within the timelines.

Such matters become rather more insurmountable, especially when the highly reserved, bashful military husband says, 'I know it! *Tum toh kar hi logi*!' (You will manage!) These are one of those melting moments for an ardent army wife, *aur ye unka wahi mazboot yakeen hain jo military wife se sab kara deti hai*! (And this is the same strong belief that makes an army wife accomplish everything!)

One such first missile of last-minute information from my husband struck me bang on recently. My husband was assigned to attend a short military course, and we had to relocate ourselves for that duration. A small accommodation was provided with a small kitchenette and basic amenities to live comfortably.

For a young couple, this is like a long holiday away from the normal run of battalion life, and generally, the married officers enjoy such courses because the only stress here remains is that of doing well in the course, and the thousand other chords of military responsibilities are cut for the time being.

Elated with this temporary place change in our regular life, we started planning our trip enthusiastically. We always preferred driving to such places, perhaps because it adds to the feeling of freedom, adventure, and the sheer joy of travelling, and because we both love long drives.

Finally, after two days of driving and a few mandatory squabbles (after all, we were married for some time now!), we reached our location.

Generally, after staying in dry, humid areas with my husband, this place looked like heaven. It was raining, it was cold, everything looked green and fresh, and the change was not only physical but visual and mental as well.

I was confident this was the place I wanted to be for the next two months. Soon, the formalities for allotting the accommodation were completed, and the keys of the quarter were handed over to us. We took a few turns from there and reached the location.

I had that same sinking feeling that every army wife has (I can vouch for that) before a new quarter is allotted. I prayed and prayed hard for it to be good. The door opened, and as always, I realized, 'God helps those who help themselves.' The same old Murphy's Law in the army was working.

I took a deep breath and decided I had to clean this place up, but for the night, I let my enthusiasm settle down and crashed to take some rest. The next morning, as the military man left for his classes, I took out my stock of pochha, jhadu, Lizol, detergent, and scrubber bought from the canteen and started my intense cleaning mission from one corner to the other. When an army wife is working on such an intense project of cleaning a government house to her standards of 'cleanness', she likes to be thoroughly equipped. The dusting cloth will be tucked into the sides of her pants, the sleeves of her kurta will be rolled up, her hair will be pulled back and tied tightly, and the pants will be rolled up to her knees. She will hold the phool jhadu in one hand and the tilli jhadu in the other, and her appearance is almost divine, her Devi roop it is!

I was busy cleaning in that divine form, but soon, the form changed to that of Kali Mata when I received a call from my soldier-turned-student husband, who rang and dropped the missile of 'we have to reach for cocktails at 19.00 hrs' and 'please *mere kapde bhi dekh lena*' (please check my clothes too). Though I was fuming with anger at this last-minute surprise, the Kali Mata form soon subsided. Like a well-groomed military wife, I understood my husband's plight, dropped my cleaning tools, and rushed to unpack my stuff, still neatly lying inside the suitcases. Without delay, I pulled out my best sari, my heels, my makeup, my perfume, my toiletries, and also the blue shirt and black trousers of my husband. I set it all nicely on a table, quickly made some tea and snacks to gobble up before we left for the cocktails, where they serve boiled veggies and thanda kheera platter (cold cucumber platter) for the first few hours before they get into some real snacks. I arranged the tea, pakoras, and cheese sandwiches made in my small kitchen with the bread, aloo (potato), and chai ki patti (tea leaves) I received as a welcome kit ration the same morning and kept it all on the dining table. Then I rushed for a quick shower, set my hair, put on my makeup, wore my sari, and abracadabra, there I was in my new Cinderella avatar as an army wife.

After so many years of being in the army with my husband, I have realized that the 'ichhadhari shakti' of the army wives lies within them and only grows with time. This shakti seeps into them from the day they start their period of complicated courtship with the military man. Unlike normal couples where the guy surprises his girlfriend with flowers and movie tickets, the most a military man can do for his girlfriend is to call back or send online cakes and flowers, if they have the network or are well-versed with online shopping sites (which was not the case in my story). That is when the girlfriend first realizes the difference between her relationship and others around. She who chooses the avatar of being 'wonder-woman' and is happy to be just the 'virtual girlfriend', satisfied with the online relationship, later qualifies to be a wife and joins our esteemed gang of military wives, while those who choose coffee and movie tickets are still roaming with their husbands near the multiplexes.

Later, this dormant inner strength of an army wife slowly grows with each passing day when life starts throwing lemons at them. I sometimes wonder if life throws so many lemons that it makes it the most popular drink of ladies here – a glass of 'nimbu paani' (lemonade)!

The role-hopper army wife generally starts her main act at 5 a.m. as the master chef at home, with her apron tied around her waist like a shield. One hand reaches for the tea leaves while the other peels almonds for her soldier husband who is leaving for the morning routine at the battalion. She quickly finishes her master chef role and shifts to the next role of being the 'housekeeper', with jhadu and duster in hand, setting the house flawlessly. In between, she will turn into a 'gardener' and check if the dry leaves are out of the pot. By around 11 a.m., she will plan to assume the role of pseudo 'combat queen', fulfilling her duties of AWWA and other welfare activities through calls or meetings. In the evening, she becomes an 'educationist' to her children and finally the role of a 'Hitler queen', who pulls out the TV plugs and mobile phones from their husbands and kids, and enforces bedtime, as she needs to get everybody ready for the following day.

This is how the poised ichhadhari army wife keeps changing her roles from one to another while maintaining her distinguished demeanour at every step!

20

The Heady Flavours of Dusk

'Shaam ka waqt' (dusk or evening) is that important hour when the fauji wife enters her multifarious chamber for experiments – her kitchen – and takes out one of the most used apparatus in every Indian household: the Chai ka Patila! Then, the *sarkari* ration *wali patti*, ration *wala doodh, chini,* and *adrak* all come together to make the super drink of a military house. No wonder they say, military *walon ki kadak chai murde mein bhi jaan daal deti hai*' (the strong tea of the military can bring the dead to life!)

The evening ritual starts with a mandatory cup of tea (the regular doodh wali Hindustani middle-class chai), often accompanied by the military bakery's ajwain biscuits – perfectly baked with no fancy packing, mostly sold open, wrapped in brown paper bags. The antiquity of such traditions still being widely followed in army setups often takes you back thirty years, reminding you of childhood days when you'd rush to the *galli wali dukaan* with some change from your mom and happily buy those namkeen to have with your evening glass of milk. Thoughts from those days of yore bring a smile to my face, and I contemplate deeply, 'How well the history is still preserved in our cantonment,' as I place the biscuits on the platter, following our ritual of evening tea at home.

We quickly catch up with each other over the day's happenings, sipping our kadak chai, sitting in the garden, hearing the chirping of the birds and the fading sound of evening games being played in the battalion, which reverberates the josh in every soul hearing it to get up and move.

Then begins the second facet of the 1800 hours ritual in a military house: getting ready for some physical activity, be it games, jogging, or walking. On one hand, the officers are off their uniforms with belts and barrettes, smartly donning crisp games attire with caps and sports shoes, riding cycles, running, and walking. At the same time, the ladies pull out their chic sportswear with smart shoes and pants, burning off those extra calories acquired from parties and impromptu baking affairs at home. This is the time when the streets of the cantonment are full of fitness enthusiasts, everyone trying hard to be in better form than the other. It is that good-vibe moment of the day where not only the officers but the ladies too join the spree of staying fit and strong.

Galvanized by the high-spirited evening norm of the army, I too got motivated. I start by downloading a sportswear shopping app on my mobile, waiting for the weekend sale to begin. After burning the midnight oil, researching the best deals, and adding about fifty sets of yoga pants, shoes, and t-shirts to the 'basket', I finally shortlist a few chic pairs and order them, waiting in anticipation for the parcels to arrive.

Meanwhile, I began preparations for my fitness regime. The first step: finding that one motivated mate who can pull you out on days when, after evening tea and biscuits, you might want to sneak back into your comfort zone, switch on Netflix, make popcorn, and glue yourself to a gripping series. So, the hunt begins for that mate. With that, other successive planning for the perfect start is deeply thought out: '*Dinner main kya banega*?' (What will be cooked for dinner?), '*Kitne baje walk start karenge*?' (When shall we start walking?), '*Kaun sa route lenge*?' (Which route shall we choose) and other associated issues.

After all that planning, I have to kick the can down the road! Finally, I break the self-created chakravyuha of household chores, step out in my newly arrived yoga pants and t-shirt, break the tags, don them, and ring my 'motivated mate' whom I had superficially entrusted with the responsibility of keeping me going.

But soon, I realize that someone else's motivation was becoming my stress. She tells me one day during our routine evening walks, 'Hey, this routine is really helping me, it seems. This t-shirt used to fit perfectly until three weeks ago, but look, now it's getting loose. I've also started a morning yoga routine, and throughout the day, it's no sugar, no carbs, only protein intake. You should also start doing yoga in the morning.'

I complete my stressful walk that day, enter the house, go straight to my room, pull out the weighing machine lying under my bed, and, not caring about the thick layer of dust over it, take off my shoes (to know the precise, right weight) and, barefoot, take that fearless step on it.

The result is hopeless. So, I leave my motivated friend with her josh and try to ignite the fire in my belly. But alas! The fire is only smouldering, *aur meri Dilli door thi abhi* (Delhi was far for me)!

Every day, after the essential 1800 hrs kadak chai, I have to deal with a major tussle of whether to be or not be on the streets to join the much-celebrated ritual celebrated by the majority of fauji janta. For a few days, reasons like '*Aaj garmi bahut hai*' (It is very hot today) or '*Aaj kuch theek nahin lag raha*' (I am not feeling well) work for me. On other days, some AWWA commitments in the evening shelter me, but one cannot run from the truth for long – I am making excuses.

There are days when, with a cup of tea in my hand, I observe the ones on the streets, and the same old internal monologue begins: '*Kaun apne ghar se nikla hai? Yeh kaise nikal jaate hain*?' (Who all have stepped out of their houses? How do they manage to get out like this?) And then I see Mrs Pant, who has a figure like a teenager. '*Arre! Inko kya zarurat hai, yeh kyun walk kar rahi hain*?' (Oh! What need do they have? Why are they walking?)

But soon, the *sota hua josh in me jag gaya*, and my baffled feelings are replaced with some cerebral clarity.

I realize, it's now or never.

Finally, I march out of my main gate in proper sports gear, mentally playing training videos with the famous tunes of Rocky Balboa, Mary Kom, and Arnold Schwarzenegger for the right motivation, and start my new-found regime towards fitness.

As I walk, I find the streets of a cantonment full of fitness enthusiasts all around. I literally meet everyone from my colony, from the officers to the ladies, and even the children happily cycling or walking. Even the courts of badminton, squash, and tennis are full, with players waiting for their turns. The whole scene in the cantonment can easily be compared to Olympic training grounds, where every player is out and training.

Seeing this, I realize 'Fauji hai, fit toh hoga hi.' But what I am actually witnessing on the streets, battalion grounds, and play areas is what goes into making the mettle in that man.

While it's natural for any human to find a million reasons to chill comfortably in their houses, it takes the right determination to pull oneself out of such comfort zones and start conditioning their bodies. And then it becomes a ritual for the whole family to follow, and when everyone participates with the same level of josh, the whole community is viewed like that.

With all these thoughts playing in my mind, I look at my smartwatch and see that I have already completed my 10,000 steps. I smile and turn back towards my home, and thus, with the setting sun, the drive to stay inspired rises within me.

21

Hum Saath Saath Hai

When I watch any Sooraj Barjatya movie, besides the contradictions and complexities of relationships, I witness the celebration of human connections irrespective of caste, creed, or status. The innocent, ignorant, wide-eyed Manohar bhaiya (like in *Maine Pyaar Kiya*), who is technically the domestic help of a mansion where all the male members of the household come home for lunch in helicopters landing on the front lawn, the ladies of the house change dresses every hour, and every evening after the grand aarti, which is more decorated than our entire Diwali decorations combined. Everybody dances and sings together, including Manohar bhaiya, and cracks jokes with 'the malik' of the house. What an ideal household. How perfect!

However, hierarchy is an important aspect of the Indian Army; it's followed at every level with utmost respect. For somebody outside the cantonment gates, it might sound very primitive, but our whole system rests on it. There has to be one voice, one decision, one plan to follow when the needful has to be done. Though analysis and plan Bs are always made in abundance, there is always one leader. Thus, at every hierarchical level in the army, a certain level of respect and decorum is maintained. We function in a much more organized manner, and every individual's responsibility is balanced by the responsibility of the other. The whole system is geared towards maintaining the ultimate stellar cosmic balance. In simple words, here Manohar bhaiya can't crack jokes with the 'malik' of the house! (especially when at work).

This balance is made stronger by the glue of love and respect for each other. One will listen to advice and suggestions put forward, and the voices are generally not curbed. A huge amount of impetus is given to the opinions of others, and to support this thought, formal events such as 'sainik sammelans', 'mess meetings', and 'welfares for the families of jawans' are organized regularly at every level in almost every battalion. These events provide a platform for all to discuss their issues and come up with suggestions, thus improving the system and enhancing functionality more inclusively.

Interestingly, in the army, these suggestions often pop up at the most unexpected times from the most unlikely individuals who believe in owning the problem and finding a way out with the best of their abilities, even if it may be the weirdest idea.

A few days before Diwali, I was returning from a shopping spree at the local market. Unlike the Diwali markets in Delhi, which is awash with various designer lamps, lights, clothing, and now even laddoos and Ganesh-ji being introduced every season, the markets at the back of beyond outposts where we live still believe in traditional items. I bought mud lamps, fragrant flower garlands, and basic Ganesh and Lakshmi idols. I had two bags full of items, so the driver thought of helping me with that. Upon getting out of the vehicle and following military courtesies, I offered him a cup of strong tea and some home-cooked snacks.

Soon, I started unpacking my shopping and arranging them for the festivities. Probably then, the driver from Banaras (who is a part of our military family) started recommending: '*Memshaib, aap phoolon wala mala dakshin wale gate main mat lagao, uttar wale gate main lagao wahan se na laxmi ghar aayegi, yahan se to shaheb ki saari Lakshmi chali na jayegi.*' (Madam, don't hang the flower garland at the south gate; hang it at the north gate. That way, Lakshmi will come into the house. If you hang it here, all of Sahib's Lakshmi will leave.)

I gave him a stiff memsahib look while I stood firmly in a state of confusion about the aesthetics for my home, and decided to clear his doubts:

'*Ramesh bhaiya, Army main kab se uttar, dakshin hone laga? Humare liye to sab dishaayein ek barabar hain.*' (Ramesh bhaiya, since when did north and south become significant in the army? For us, all directions are equal.)

Ramesh bhaiya nodded in agreement. '*Woh to sahi bola, madam, aap.*' (Rightly said, madam.)

During one extreme summer afternoon, another soldier came home to deliver some important files to the military man and suggested covering the whole roof with dry hay, as they do in their villages, to keep the house cooler in summer. I had to politely convince him to avoid such weird ideas. Another time, during the monsoon, it started raining. Someone recommended placing a tawa upside-down in the front lawn of the mess to stop the rain, as they do in their village to avoid excessive rain during the farming season!

Frankly, at times it did work! But what I strongly feel is that it's often the confidence and positivity that manifest and make things work at their best.

However, the most important challenge in the army is to develop an ability to take everybody along and respect each other's individuality. This may seem like strange advice based on archaic beliefs to me, but for some, it is their reality – an absolute they have grown up with, imparted by important figures in their lives, and carried deep within their memories. They continue to believe in it, even if they are physically, mentally, and emotionally distant from that time and place. It's surprising that when you stay in a close-knit establishment like ours, where both jawans and officers come from varied backgrounds of culture, creed, religion, occupation, and position, one can only imagine the amount of tolerance the establishment nurtures for the varied views emerging from such an intensive amalgamation.

Finally, we have realized as a society that we are just the residues of a cosmic clash and there is no ultimate rulebook in life. Until we learn to coexist with everything that nature has provided us, and let go of the inconsequential aspects of power, money, and position, we may never grow as humankind.

22

Living the Memsahib Image

In India, 'aunty' is not merely a polite reference for women; it carries several implied meanings. It often suggests an image of 'I know it all.' Comments like '*Yeh aunty hai!*' (She is an aunty!) imply that 'she knows it all,' regardless of the dictionary definition. It can refer to someone who is ageing, someone who has contributed to the world's population, someone following outdated fashion, or often, it's just used to annoy someone and get a reaction. The word is used differently across various contexts, implying different things.

In the army, however, you may be just twenty-five years old, married to 'hum-umar' military man, but you will instantly be dubbed 'aunty' by nearly every child in the cantonment – even if that 'child' is the same age as you, as long as they're unmarried.

In ordinary circumstances, this might anger you, and you

might want to correct the other person. But in a military setup, when you are someone's wife, this title is nothing less than a mark of respect from the younger generation. For a young, vibrant woman, being addressed this way in an army setup might be hard to swallow, especially when you're bubbling with youthful energy and feeling on top of the world. Such suffixes may feel like a sudden fall to the ground, hitting you hard – until you learn that this title is actually a safety belt, keeping you grounded and protected while you navigate the limitless horizons of military life.

From the day I married my military man, despite all the wonderful changes I experienced, solemn responsibilities awaited me, to be shouldered alongside my husband. While these responsibilities gave me wings to fly, they also came with certain conditions. On a broader level, these conditions were traditions that intricately shaped me as an army wife. As I embraced these traditions, I evolved beyond just being an army wife; I became a 'Memsahib', a title more profound than just a respectful address.

The concept of 'memsahib' originated during colonial India, where the term was primarily used for foreign women of high social status, especially the wives of British officers. After the British left, and the Indian armed forces took over the country's defence responsibilities, many of the British ways of functioning were adopted, including the use of the term 'memsahib'. The word is widely used to refer to the wives of Indian Army officers and junior commissioned officers. To this day, we continue this tradition, using it as a mark of respect and grace towards army wives. Every battalion idolizes its 'memsahibs' as symbols of purity, warmth, tolerance, and support. She is like the mother of the battalion, and all regard her with this notion in mind.

Before my army life, I was a reckless soul in Delhi, roaming around the city with a bag full of aspirations. Coffee, shopping, work, and weekend splurges were the norm. My world revolved around a close-knit circle of friends and family. From festivals to birthdays, I sailed through life on a steady course, with little change, and safe, predictable events. Even random ideas like social work or adoption would often strike me after reading an intriguing newspaper column or witnessing a candle march at India Gate. But by evening, the allure of urban life and its comforts would usually prevail over these thoughts.

Landing in the military as the wife of a soldier brought a lot of personal growth. As mentioned earlier, the image of an army wife is like that of a 'mother' to the battalion, and one has to live up to that image on various levels. The challenges were immense, especially when emotional needs arose. There were times when I was the only woman in the operating theatre, providing comfort to the families of soldiers. They trusted me deeply, believing that nothing could go wrong with their memsahib by their side.

Numerous occasions in army life required me to provide motivation and courage. As their respected memsahib, my words instilled hope in their lives. I could see it so clearly in their glistening eyes as they listened intently when I encouraged them to complete their studies or spoke about women's health and hygiene. The trust they had in this so-called 'memsahib' image was palpable.

Most of these soldiers' families come from rural India, where they have never received the motivation they longed for. It could be something as simple as speaking their minds or something as significant as chasing and fulfilling their dreams. Many soldiers' wives have completed their education, nurtured their talents, enjoyed their hobbies, and even turned into entrepreneurs – thanks to army welfare ventures and the constant encouragement from a memsahib who cared enough to help them climb the ladder of life.

Balancing the roles of a memsahib in the battalion and an involved wife at home with my own set of challenges and family responsibilities, I realized that a true army wife is nothing less than a hero working in the background. At home, she is like a genie, transforming everything into beauty. Officially, as a memsahib, she not only supports the wives of all the soldiers under her husband's command emotionally and mentally but also contributes to building bonds of solidarity, unity, and compassion. These bonds don't just bind the soldiers; they extend to their families and children, often growing thicker than blood.

What's most interesting is that such feelings come naturally to the men who are trained to live and die together. But when wives come into this setup, simply because they chose to marry men in uniform, and then wholeheartedly follow the army's traditions and responsibilities, it's a remarkable show of character.

In today's world, where women are pursuing enterprising careers, earning large salaries, enjoying their independence, and living life on their own terms, we also have women from similar backgrounds joining the army and contributing immensely. Their reward is often a tight hug, a bright smile, or a twinkle in the eyes of a woman or child who longed for the right motivation or support in life. I strongly believe that lifting each other up is the greatest karma and the most significant sense of accomplishment. The army provides its ladies with this enormous opportunity in life, and we are forever indebted.

On a lighter note, maintaining such an aura requires not only immense compassion and a sense of responsibility but also the right demeanour. Thankfully, the sari, the national dress of India for women, performs that nine-yard miracle every time.

The moment an army wife wraps a sari, accentuates the look with a string of pearls around her neck, puts on sunglasses to hold back her hair, and places a bindi on her forehead, she transforms from a regular, sweet married lady into a woman of substance – a memsahib!

It almost feels like a superhero transformation, where donning the superhero suit instantly empowers you to defeat even the mightiest foes. Similarly, the sari works its magic on an army wife. The best part is that this pseudo-superhero suit comes in various styles, catering to her feminine senses as well. From Chanderi to Maheshwari, Kota, silks, cottons, and more, the wide range of options helps in creating the memsahib aura and adds that extra spark.

23

Ambrosia

'Kesar Kashmir ka', *'Badaam Kabul ka'*, *'Pani RO ka,'*, *'Seb Shimla ka'* ...*'daru fauji ki' duniya bhar mein mashoor hai.* (Just as 'kesar from Kashmir', 'almonds from Kabul', 'RO water', and 'apples from Shimla' are renowned, 'the alcohol of a soldier' is famous around the world.)

A fauji's love of collecting 'alcohol bottles' beggars belief. When a guest comes to a military house, in addition to the collection of fine porcelain, crochet or artefacts placed around the house, a true military couple will take immense pride in showing their bar section which the husband contributes to building up the collection, while his better half enhances the look and feel by working on the interiors to create the perfect ambience at the most important corner of the home.

This is the only domestic affair of my house where the military man was totally involved. He is thrilled and takes

In a military home, every bottle gets a salute on arrival

immense pride in showing the bar collection, which could rival any opulent spirit shop. Sometimes, the suspicious wife in me even wonders where my military man finds the funds to afford such fancy bottles. Unlike the apps I have downloaded on my phone, I don't think there's any online shopping app offering seasonal discounts on spirits. My suspicions stay unanswered, but who cares when you see, for a change, a smiling, stress-free military husband standing behind the bar admiring his rare collectibles?

Like building any exclusive collection, a lot of time, planning, and money are invested. A lot of thought goes up in building a prime collection. The overworked military man of my house who apparently has no time to involve himself in anything household-related, is always game to invest his leftover energies by 'nurturing his hobby'.

With a glass of scotch in his hand and jazz in the background, he says in a deep voice, 'There's something more I want to do in life.'

I nod while gulping my glass of wine, knowing that it's the cocktail of leisure, middle age, and scotch that leads to such realizations in life! However, being a fauji's wife, I had to stand by my husband shoulder to shoulder and contribute generously to this futile dialogue. Therefore, the motivating wife in me suggests, 'Why don't you take up some hobby?'

A long pause follows, and soon, after a lot of debate, we finally realize that he is one of those faujis 'who doesn't have any hobby'. But I also realize soon that such faujis have a unanimous hobby, and that is to research on 'liquor bottles' – topics such as '*kitne ki milti*' (how much does it cost?), '*kahan milti hai*' (where can it be found?) really light up their lives.

To my surprise, such intense discussions among the fauji bhais can dilute the whole concept of 'time', and it can go on for hours and hours at night especially after dinner. In those moments, somehow, the 'alcoholic' cells in his body take over the deep-seated, omnipresent 'sleepoholic' ones. With every beep of the message lying on the other side of the bed, I felt the discussions growing more and more intense, with variables of price and place being compared. Some enthusiastic 'bhais' even pluck up the courage to call such unearthly hours for more clarity. Often, such deep conferences by the husbands can only be brought to an end by a ballistic, half-asleep wife on the other side of the bed. And it happened in this case as well; finally, my patience gave way, and I could take no more 'gyaan' on liquor. I roared from my side of the bed, and that was it; the research work ended.

Finally, with more discussions on which bottles to buy with the 'research and development' group of friends, the military man of the house bought some unique military liquor bottles from a distant station canteen. The bhai sending the consignment took all precautionary measures to ensure not even one bottle broke and the hard-earned money of his 'bhai' wasn't wasted. This involved a wooden box tightly wrapped in layers of hessian cloth, gatta, and bubble wrap, and just like an Egyptian mummy the bottles were laid inside the wooden box with extra hay all around them.

The day the box reached our house, an evening was planned with my military man's in-station bhais for the 'opening ceremony' of this 'mummy box' that would fill the cantonment with josh. Each bottle was taken out and unwrapped with utmost diligence. The whole process of setting up the bar with these bottles seemed to me nothing less than a well-organized military exercise, where one friend was removing the layers, another was dusting, and the last one was placing the bottles inside the bar carefully. I kept observing all of them while preparing snacks from the kitchen and could only be amazed.

After two months of my husband's riveted look admiring his bar, finally he spoke. ' We must try this bottle,' he said, pulling out a tall, slender turquoise blue bottle with something written on it in Russian (at least it looked Russian).

'Of course! We must,' I agreed, as I was eager to taste such an expensive drink and understand why these men were so serious about it.

Without any further delay, the military man called up his other 'connoisseur' friends from the adjacent block, and with that, the grand opening ceremony of the bottle was under way. After all the necessary arrangements of the ice cubes, scotch glasses (whipped and dried thrice), a platter of fruits, cheese, and snacks were laid, the military man of the house walked towards the bar, held the bottle, and to my amazement, gave a formal speech on the procurement of the bottle. Finally, when the drinks were poured into the glasses with ice cubes, I could feel the childlike thrill among my guests and my military man. We all clinked our glasses, praying for the health and happiness of all, and took the first sip.

As the spirit went down my throat, a very musty taste unfolded on my palate. I was baffled by it and wondered if

I should spit it out. But as I read the expression of the others around, I knew there was something fishy. I asked my military man, who looked confused, 'Does it taste like this?'

He too, not looking too happy with the results, replied honestly, 'I think it's spoiled,' to which one of his very enthusiastic research and development friends added, '*Arre! Nahin! Iska taste hi aisa hota hai.*' (No, this tastes like this.)

The other also agreed, '*Haan, itni mehngi hai, aise thodi karab ho jayegi.*' (This is so costly. It will not get bad so easily.)

Then, with the mutual consent of all the bhais, it was unanimously agreed that '*sharab kabhi karab nahin ho sakti.*' (That would translate to wine never goes bad, but like most translations, the fizz gets lost in translation – there is no way that the rhyme scheme of sharab and kharab can be rendered in English.)

The party continued till the whole bottle was downed, and nobody even questioned about how it tasted the second time.

The next morning, life returned to its normal course, with the military man back in action with none of the night's revelries showing. On the other hand, the frugal army wife element in me was busy planning to make use of the heap of empty bottles from the party; I cheerfully examined them all and thereafter stacked them according to their usage. Wasting no time, I called up my friend, another army officer's wife, who was an expert in decoupage. I selected two bottles of Jack Daniel's and two bottles of Morpheus brandy, washed, cleaned, and dried them properly.

Finally, I gave her a call and requested her to decoupage these bottles, to which she replied, '*Haan, haan, tu bhej de saare bottles. Sham ko aake tissue select kar lena.* (Yeah, yeah, send all the bottles. Come in the evening to select the tissue.) I will put a shade and holder over them; you can use them as lamps as well. Come over for tea in the evening, and I will show you what I have made.'

Bingo! I instantly wrapped those bottles, put them in a bag, and sent them to her place for the makeovers.

After that, with the remaining six beer bottles, I decided to try out my horticulture skills. I had downloaded a few images from Pinterest and saw similar empty drinks bottles beautifully decorated with jute threads, marbles, and money plant saplings (perhaps, the creativity of some alcoholic wreck's wife!), so I decided to recreate that look with a few variations. As I had no marbles and no patience to glue those jute threads around the bottle, I decided to keep it simple – just the bottle, water, and the sapling! I pondered – bottles I had enough, water was in the tank, the only thing I needed was the money plant sapling (I have always believed in plants with purpose; it should either give fruit, shade, medicine, or good luck). I knew that money plants bring a lot of good fortune and money, but the issue was I believed in the myth that it only does so if it has been plucked from someone else's garden and that too without their knowledge!

I started on this mission and took out my car, driving in search of money plants! Strongly believing that it will bring good fortune to me, I entered the gates of a nearby colony and finally saw the house of Mrs Shaw to my left. Mrs Shaw was known all through the cantonment for her passion for gardening. I quietly parked my car under the neem tree behind the bougainvillaea bush, walked over, and plucked a few saplings of money plant hanging from her main door. Thereafter, walking on eggs, I moved towards the car and drove back to my home, almost surviving a heart attack for what I had just done.

After two weeks, on one of the free weekends, the military man was in the house enjoying the evening, listening to Kishore Kumar songs while admiring his teeming bar and swiftly adjusting the bottles for better display. While I was sitting on the bar stool reading my book and waiting for my drink, I asked him to switch on the lamps placed on the pet table with the clear bottle of glowing money plant sapling kept on the side. As usual, after struggling to find the button, he finally switched the lamp on and instantly said, 'What a beautiful set-up! *Yeh lamp kab liya*?' (When did you buy this lamp?) I glanced at the military man from the bar counter, took a deep breath, and said, '*Meri drink bana rahe ho*?' (Are you making my drink?)

24

Sab 'Tik Tok Hain': English, Army-style

Of all the things the British took away from India, they could never take away the inborn attitude of 'resilience' from us. 'Resilience' – one of the finest qualities in mankind – which impels us to bounce back, adapt, fight, and withstand any adversities life throws our way. We have grown as a nation over these years across all sectors and today have emerged as an eminent nation on the world map.

Undoubtedly, we Indians have an extraordinary ability to survive in any situation. Not only do we survive, we also diligently work to triumph over it. Without delving into the incredible list of far-reaching accomplishments of our country, let me just mention the smallest Indian vendor, who sells so-called Chinese momos from his stall under a tree, and how he alters the flavours to match the Indian palate and thus increase his sales. That's the art of survival we master. We twist and turn, adjust, and find our way through almost any situation.

I was surprised to witness a variety available in a simple thing like a momo during one of my latest visits to Delhi. I had a chance to visit my favourite spot in the city and was caught off-guard by the wide range of flavours he had – Maggie, achari, tandoori, rajma. Lately, I discovered that he had taken a leap and started offering Indian-flavoured sushis as well, knowing that people are gradually moving towards it from the same old momos! That's having business foresightedness! Let me take a moment to salute this extraordinary spirit of 'resilience' in my favourite momo vendor.

There are plenty of such resilient souls in the army too! As we all know, the Indian army is influenced by the traditions of a British army to quite an extent (all thanks to the 200 years of British Raj). Other than the work culture, hierarchical distinctions, mannerisms, etc., a widely influenced segment is 'The Language'. In the army, it is considered formal and more military-like to converse in English. When a military man speaks formally, especially during presentations, the sentence formations have to be very strict with limited words, and after every word, there is sometimes a pause that makes it sound more like an automated robot. The syntax of the sentences is so combatant in nature that it automatically sounds mechanized, as if a robot were in conversation with you.

Not only the officers and soldiers but the ladies also adopt this exclusively transformed Indian Army angrezi in their day-to-day life. These military men have so exceptionally army-fied a few words of Shakespearean English that it would make even

Shakespeare doubt whether he ever composed them! Moreover, with the abundance of confidence in military personnel, they speak these words with so much conviction that, for a moment, you start doubting your own linguistic knowledge.

One such doubt crept into my mind one fine day, when I started using my husband's phone.

Just for some friendly additional information for all my male readers, the moment a husband's phone reaches a wife's hand, the dormant 'James Bond' genes in her awaken immediately! (This particular feature applies to every man on this planet and not restricted only to men of the Indian Army.)

In the blink of an eye, I checked his call records, photos, and emails and then reached the message section. Before guilt about such actions begins to weigh on your heart, let me give you some sisterly advice.

Such acts of surveillance are completely normal, and a faithful wife has every legitimate right to do so! (This particular feature is also for the whole womankind and not applicable to Indian wives only.)

During the cursory reading of the messages in his phone, one particular message piqued my attention. I saw that this one particular sender sends a similar message every day at the same time! I scrolled up and down and then down up. 'This is not normal,' the James Bond in me asserted. Is my husband a spy? Is he using code language? Is he working for some secret agency? All sorts of doubts started hovering in my mind; I opened the message again, squinted my eyes in suspicion, and read the lines carefully: 'Sahib, all Tik Tok hai' and then the next day again 'Sahib, all Tik Tok hai' and then the following day again 'Sahib, all 41 Tik Tok hai'. The same message was sent at the same time every day by the same number!

All social media is banned for army personnel for security reasons; what 'Tik Tok' were they mentioning in this chat? Was this some code language? Was he using the TikTok app secretly? Wasn't it banned in India? I couldn't take it anymore; I had to find out what was brewing in my house. Stirring up the fauji wife's Nari Shakti component in me, I bombarded my unguarded husband with all the questions.

Who are you? For whom do you work, and who is sending you these messages? What is the code language? What does TikTok mean? I know it is banned in India. What's happening in this house? Are we safe?'

He, in a total state of shock, calmed me down and very patiently heard my whole investigation, and then, when I ended, he rolled down laughing hysterically; I was totally baffled! What's wrong with this man?

He very calmly explained, 'This is part of the daily report I get from the battalion. Sipahi Ram Prasad sends it to me.'

'And what is this Tik Tok thing all about?'

The military man replied, 'It's not Tik Tok, dear! He means "Thik Thak", sab theek thaak hai, everything is well, that is what he means when he writes that. And don't you know we generally follow Roman English, where we communicate in Hindi but use the English script? It's in Roman, so maybe some spelling mistakes here and there.'

I was completely rattled and felt so embarrassed; however, in my defence, I left a sarcastic remark, '*Tum aur tumhari fauz*! (You and your army) ... I wonder if Romans even know how their language is being slaughtered by you fellows,' and left the room sheepishly.

As the years went on, I became more and more 'resilient' in the army, and besides all the other rituals and customs which I learnt through the years, I too adopted the conventional angrezi of the fauz.

So now when the washerman says, '*Memsahab! Sahab ki combined dress press kar du*?' (Ma'am, shall I iron sir's combined dress) I know he means, '*Sahab ki combat dress press kar du*?' (Shall I iron sahab's combat dress?)

When the gardener says, '*Memsahib! Garden fence ko cover karne ke liye hessian cloth chahiye*' (Madam! We need hessian cloth to cover the garden fence), I knew he means, '*Garden main hessian cloth chahiye*' (Hessian cloth is needed for the garden).

If the jawan says, '*Sahib galti ka koi chance nahin main bilkul "fauxed" tha*' (There is no chance of mistake I was 'fauxed'), it means that 'he was totally focused'.

And the most widely used angrezi word in the fauj, 'condemnation', is spelled in the most unimaginable way which I won't mention but leave to your imaginations.

During the course of being with my husband, I kept adopting these lingos and adding to the exclusive collection of fauji linguistics, and still, at times, I fail to understand many such 'code words' in fauzi angrezi. However, I instantly remember my 'Tik Tok' experience and presume '*iska kuch matlab toh zaroor hoga*' and carry on.

I realized that in our society, it is generally taken as a commonplace, ordinary expression, used frequently when discussing the attributes of our developing country. However, we often fail to fully grasp that such fragments of impeccable traits collectively become the hallmark qualities that bind our great nation as one of the largest democracies in the world.

The chain of thoughts hovering in my mind was interrupted by the loud 'Jai Shri Krishna' as the clock struck 12, and finally, Gopal was born. The baby was offered 'chhappan bhog', and the whole jhula was vibrantly decorated with the best flowers from our gardens. All of us stood to take the blessings and prasad, and within a few minutes, the 'Sarv Dharm Sthal' was tidied up, and the bhajan mandli packed up, all ready for the morning parade.

After the whole celebration, we returned to the house, contented and at peace. While changing my sari, I continued thinking of the whole experience of the 'Sarv Dharm Sthal' and concluded, 'This must be the ultimate superpower guiding our nation, not the individual planning of our million gods, but the godlike qualities in us that keep us together, growing, and progressing towards a better tomorrow.'

When you live such a tough life, where every moment is uncertain and full of pressure, you might need a little extra blessing and protection from 'The One' for your loved ones. And because of the belief in 'the more, the merrier', why rely on just 'The One' when we have 'The One in Many and the Many in One' to shield us?

26

Raag Fauj

Irrespective of all the big and small varied aspects of the army, there are a few common golden threads which bind all faujis together, and surprisingly, music is a prime one on the list. You will be pleasantly surprised to read that nearly 99 percent of the faujis are music lovers and can sing! (Especially after a drink).

Apparently, their choice of songs also remains the same and they would absolutely not mind singing the same song at every party but with different levels of emotions and intensity, as this remains directly proportional to the number of drinks they have had and which is in turn inversely proportional to the amount of work they have done on that day. So logically, there is a pattern they follow just like in their work; after all, their minds are trained like that.

If the soldier has had a tough day, he will drink less and

therefore may not sing at all. However, if he has had a light day (if the boss has not berated him for something), he will enjoy his drink and pour all his emotions and intensities into his singing.

This talent is not just restricted to the officer class; the soldiers too are abundantly endowed with it. Most of the best singers in the troop are from the North East and their swag is at a different level. The moment they put aside their rifles and pick up the guitar and strum those strings, they look no less than rock stars.

One would be blown away seeing the contrast in these sober and staid men doing all strenuous and critical work during the day – loading tanks with ammunition, for example – and the same men holding the mic singing Bryan Adams or Kishore Kumar songs in the evening. I witnessed this stark difference in the personality of a soldier during one of my monthly visits to the battalion canteen where I get the basic household stuff for the month.

Every time I entered the canteen, there was this soldier I found working at the billing counter. He was a fair, short guy with small eyes and would never meet my gaze; even when I asked for any details, he would politely look down and reply. Once, I walked up to him for some clarity on a product. He was sitting straight at the billing counter and typing vigorously on the sales computer.

I asked, 'Don't you have olive oil?'

He quickly checked his computer and in very soft incoherent Hindi replied in his trademark style, looking down towards the shelf of the wooden counter, 'Ma'am I don't have it at the moment. I will bring it next month.'

I continued with my shopping and finally went back to him for the final billing. He, in his usual manner, didn't utter a single extra word, finished the billing formality, handed me the bill, wished 'Namaste ma'am', and handed over the stuff.

Later in the week, we had to attend a cocktail party in the mess. I entered the venue together with the military man, formally dressed, and then split into our own groups of friends. Talking about a typical army party setup, you would find a bar (sometimes more than one depending on the strength), an AV screen for presentations or games, a few T-stands with salted chips and peanuts (especially kept for the young officers), chairs and sofas with petite tables, fan (depending on the weather) and a jazz band (for sure!).

Now, when I say a 'jazz band', don't compare it with those at chic South Delhi restaurants where a beautiful woman clad in a sexy gown with curly hair would be the lead singer. She will have that deep, melodic, flexible tone and so much charm to melt every heart listening to her, her team with jazzy trumpets and saxophones to add to her spell, and they will swing you to the vintage world of art, music, and matured wine. On the contrary, here in the fauj, the only criteria to qualify as a jazz band is if you can sing confidently or play an instrument, even if only a little. There is no embargo in the selection of the instrument as well; unlike in civil, where a jazz band consists of all Western instruments, in a fauji jazz band, anything will work.

In the daytime, these fauji jazz band members may be found under a tank all soaked in grease and oil repairing a tank or drenched in sweat and oil at the battalion langar frying puris, or practising at the firing ranges in scorching heat knocking down every single target. But if in the evening they are picked by the senior and tasked to be a part of the jazz band, they will transform into that too in seconds.

Sometimes the lead singer, unlike the sexy jazz singer in civil, can be a six-foot Khalsa with a thick beard and eyebrows looking more like a Rambo than a musician. But then a book cannot be judged by its cover, and the show must go on – and it better go on flawlessly if it's a fauji show!

That evening, clad in my new crepe sari with a glass of gin with tonic water in one hand and paneer tikka in the other, I was busy conversing with my battalion ladies when I heard a melodious voice singing my favourite Ed Sheeran number. It made me turn and fall silent. The voice was so captivating that I could feel the ripple in the crowd, everyone quietly wrapping up the conversation and moving towards the 'jazz band'. I too moved with my girl gang and realized that this was none other than the same North Eastern lance naik from the canteen, who seldom spoke. Here he was, standing with the jazz band holding the guitar and singing English numbers flawlessly.

I was amazed. After the song, everyone applauded and I walked up to him with my husband to compliment the team. While my husband shook hands with them and said 'very good' to all of them, I too, in my exuberance, said to the familiar face, 'You have sung really well.' He just smiled formally and replied looking down towards the lawn grass, 'Thank you ma'am.' I moved back to the party with the firm thought that 'definitely!' a book cannot be judged by its cover.

The party kept rolling and slowly everyone was pulled to sing. I was glad to see all the officers enjoy those light moments, laughing and cheering for each other. They looked relaxed; it was a wonderful change of sight from the normal job atmosphere.

The only thing that baffled me was witnessing this alteration in their personality. Absolutely serious individuals who had been battle-hardened, arguing like children, laughing as if there was no care in the world, and just not ready to leave that mic.

These same set of officers, under normal circumstances, would hardly speak, stay formal, and limit their conversation to very 'officer-like' topics with us ladies. For a newcomer like me to witness such a sight, these officers squabbling over holding on to that silly 'mic' – and that too, what for? To sing those endless Kishore Kumar numbers in the most arrhythmic irregular beats! Songs such as 'Gulabi Akhein Jo Teri Dekhi,' 'Musafir Hu Yaaron,' and 'Meri Sapno Ki Rani Kab Aayegi Tu' have become Indian Army party anthems. Somehow the choices of songs revolve around these few songs. Even today, after spending more than a decade in the army as a military wife, I still hear them being sung with the same fervour as I heard it on that day. It was yet another realization that there is much more to these military men than what we just see, or if I may say, what they show.

27

The Academic Battleground

'*Zindagi har gadi ek nayi jung hai, jeet jayenge hum (fauz main) jeet jayenge hum, agar (fauz) ki padaai sang hai*!'

(Life is a new battle every moment, we will win [in the army], we will win, if [the army's] education is with us!)

Among many soldiers who join the Indian Army in anticipation of living a life full of adventure and challenges, there are a few who also choose it for one more added purpose: '*fauj main padai nahin hogi*' (there won't be any studying in the army). Little do they know what awaits them in their careers.

As we already know, a soldier's life is full of challenges and uncertainties, but what we don't know is that his military career is full of 'padai', the studyholism in the military operates at an entirely different level.

At every stage of a military career, officers as well as the men have to go through a series of certifications or military courses, as they are popularly called, wherein they are taught the tactical know-how of military operations and warfare and are finally tested through a tough examination. The merits acquired in these courses have a direct impact on their careers; therefore, it is expected of every soldier to be attentive and perform well in all the courses to keep rising and growing in the service.

Though the performance pressure during such courses weighs heavily on the men in uniform, what they also look for is a time to replenish their bonds with their peers (the bhais), and the change which comes in their module of work. Generally during the courses they do away with the 5 a.m. physical training and can laze around in bed for twenty minutes more. They have to spend the day in their classrooms studying, making presentations or researching on a military paper rather than being in the firing ranges in scorching heat hearing the muzzle blasts or lying greased under the tank. Also, at nights they can probably have dinners at ease with their friends in restaurants or order food in their rooms rather than going to the mess dining rooms in formals with belts and leather shoes.

Yes! The places or centres where these courses are conducted offer another welcome change; most of the times the locations of these courses are well known! This in itself is a big change for military ears, '*ki jagah ka naam suna hua hai*' (we have heard about the place). Pune and Indore are among the most popular ones. Therefore, on weekends or on a leisurely day, evenings can be spent with peers dining or just chilling in or around these towns, which is better than what is typically envisaged for military men.

The young lieutenants and captains, who are generally around the age group of twenty-three to twenty-six, are the ones who capitalize on this the maximum. During the course, with no seniors around them to make decisions on their behalf, the young lads, like any energetic soul with bubbling hormones in their body, live a bit of city life, eat, shop, and make girlfriends. The lot of married officers however use this time more prudently! With the maturity attained through age and service bracket, they now know the importance of performing well in their careers; therefore, their focus will not deviate too much from the course.

One such opportunity knocked at the doors of our fate after a few years of our marriage, and I could tell my friends that '*hum bhi course attend karne jaa rahe hain*' (we will also be attending the course). We had to pack for the duration we would be out of our homes. (This was one odd military course where wives were allowed, and thank god for that.) While doing so, I witnessed how my sincere soldier at home went about packing the essentials. He was all charged up and focused on accepting the challenges of a military course, and the whole preparation he was undertaking was quite a sight. He filled the boxes and cartons with military books of all sizes, an infinite number of pens and pencils (as he still prefers writing over typing), erasers, maps, staplers, file pins, whitener, A4 sheets, and whatnot. I had a feeling that he had bought the whole stationery shop. Astonished by the meticulous planning, I thought of reminding him politely, '*Apne kapde bhi rakh lena*!' (Keep your clothes too!)

'Can you adjust that in your suitcase? There's no space here,' he replied without looking towards me, staying engrossed in piling his military books.

'Ok! I will adjust,' I replied, disappointed, as I was already short of space, as always, in my suitcase.

He instantly handed me one pair of jeans, one pair of trousers, one T-shirt, and one formal shirt and said, '*Inhe adjust kar lena, please. Mere fauji kapde box main aa jayenge.*' (Please adjust these, my army clothes will fit in this box.)

I looked at those four pairs of clothes in my hand, nodded in agreement and left the room. It's still a mystery how a man can survive with only four pairs of clothes, broadly in shades of blue and black, but then I chose to leave those mysteries aside, squeezed those four sets into one corner of my suitcase and continued to stuff my 'if need be' set of clothes religiously into my brand-new pink suitcase I had picked from the canteen the morning before.

The next two days were spent on the road, and after driving for some 1000 km we reached our destination – another cantonment but in a new and famous city. Everything looked quite organized. We got the married accommodation there, which had a small kitchenette attached, one living room, one bedroom, and the toilets. It was furnished with basic amenities like a fridge, TV, and microwave. It all looked like a perfect getaway for a young couple like us.

I, in my usual high spirits, started unpacking, while the military man started setting up the study corner. Later in the evening, when I was still busy setting up the kitchen, I saw my husband entering with piles of more books and files, a desktop computer, and a printer, which was part of the course material provided to all student officers. He then finally arranged them all around his study table and placed a photo of Hanuman-ji on one side of the table with an agarbatti stand.

Finally, tired of arranging the temporary abode, we looked at each other and knew what we wanted at that moment to replenish our sinking spirits – a cup of garam chai! Without wasting time, I prepared it and joined him back for some gupshup.

'Is there any good place nearby? When are we going to the waterfall? I have heard a lot about it,' I inquired.

'We will go, we will definitely go one day,' my husband replied, and I instantly knew from that now-familiar tone of his 'that we are not going'.

'You must find time, we are on a course, we must go for sure,' I asserted.

'I am on the course, which is why I'm saying let's see how much time we get. I am still on duty, not on vacation.'

In the subsequent days, more light was thrown on this, and it was evident to me soon that this was a sabbatical period for a competitive military course and not a bolt for freedom.

I could relate the general environment of our house to those situations when children have board exams. The military man of the house would leave with a leather satchel around 8 a.m. for the classes and would be back for lunch. In the evenings, the classes would run till almost 8 at night. He would often be found doing his assignments in the corner of the room, which became the study corner of the house, or be making presentations, working with maps, or studying for the next day's exams.

Not only did my husband change into a student here, but I also automatically transformed into a 'mummy' from a wife. One night I saw the poor guy studying late into the night in the study corner of the house, rubbing his eyes and struggling to stay awake but rigorously filling pages. I immediately jumped out of my bed and instantly stood next to him with a hot mug of Horlicks.

'Drink this. My mom used to make it for me during exams. It will help you stay awake. Drink up.'

Without wasting a second, he gulped it down as if it was what he had been waiting for. In the days that followed, my 'mummy' trait was at its peak.

I used to set the alarm and wake the student officer in the house. Garam chai was replaced with milk and almonds, and the TV was completely shut during study hours. However, I was also aware that I was his wife and that I should confuse him with my role reversals. Therefore, I pulled myself out of this self-imposed role and focused on finding out what to do now that my husband was busy with the course.

It was then that I discovered the various hobby classes being run by senior military wives for the ladies who join their husbands during the course. Giving up the 'mummy' role, I quickly enrolled myself in the baking classes and thus commenced my long-awaited baking journey in the army.

Over the next few days, the atmosphere in the house was completely knowledge-intensive. In one corner, the military man and student officer was deeply engrossed in his intense studies, while in the other, I struggled to master the multiple cake and pastry recipes from my baking classes. Both made notes and struggled to comprehend the endless printouts handed out by our respective centres of learning.

The second phase began for us both soon after a month of this endless learning. It was time for action, and we had to prove our mettle. The second phase demanded the application of all the theories we had acquired over these days. I began my baking experiments in the kitchen, and simultaneously, the assessment process started for the military man. Long precious hours were spent in our individual battlefields – me experimenting with the recipes I had learned, and he with his books and assignments. Often, during short breaks, we enjoyed tasting fresh bakes from my kitchen, and finally, we would return to our respective tasks after critically analysing his exam preparation and my cake and dessert preparations.

I felt that with each passing day, both of us gained a lot as individuals and felt well-equipped for our future as a military couple. I not only excelled in baking but also learned of exclusive desserts from veteran ladies of the Indian Army, passed down as part of the military wife legacy from one generation to the next. I felt blessed to be in such graceful company and emerged more accomplished.

For the military man, too, it was an eye-opening moment when he realized that the military is not just about wearing uniforms and handling guns and tanks, but involves a lot of strategy, planning, and thinking at every stage. The extensive studies, complex projects, endless assignments, and in-depth discussions in the course expanded his perspective and deepened his understanding of the organization.

The last day of the course had to be special for everyone, and for that, my friends – whom I met during baking classes and later bonded with over countless cups of coffee while our husbands were busy with their classes – and I planned to make it memorable for our student husbands. Like in our college days, we 'sophisticated' and 'cultured' ladies ventured through the narrow lanes of the market on our colourful scooters in search of party supplies. As usual, we haggled, bargained, and explored all options to make our farewell party a success.

We planned for almost everything – from balloons to paper plates and games to party poppers. Snacks were outsourced to a nearby canteen, but the only issue we faced was with the cake. We had all attended a four-week class on baking, but none of us were confident enough to bake one for the party. Finally, after extensive discussion, it dawn on us that it would only be our military husbands eating the cake. And they wouldn't be able to tell the difference between sugar and salt if not told. They can eat anything and everything! So, we decided to proceed with our cake-baking experiment for the party. We made a chocolate cake, and when it turned out well, our confidence soared, and we decided to focus on its appearance. We took out our notes on icing the cake and made small rosettes on top of it. When this was successful, we used different colours and finally wrote a special message for the men in uniform.

It all came out perfectly, and then, finally, when the men in uniform returned in the evening with their course results, it reminded me of how as students we used to proudly walk back home and hand over our mark sheets to our parents, who would wait in anticipation. Then, in the evening, we used to celebrate with cakes and ice creams. The 'mummy' in me popped up again, and I felt immensely proud of the military man in the house. I wanted to celebrate his achievements and the relentless effort he put into his studies. So, we dressed up, ordered snacks, turned on the music, and let our hair down.

Finally, after hours of dancing and cheering for our husbands, we remembered that we too had a trophy waiting in the refrigerator – the cake we had made. It was then presented to our husbands, who, like us, were equally surprised and couldn't believe we had actually made it. It was a moment to celebrate each other and realize once again that the army is an organization where both husband and wife learn and grow together.

28

Of No Fixed Address

Generally, after staying at one station for about two years, we receive new postings. Every time I pack up my home, this song plays in the background of my mind, which is preoccupied with packing countless black boxes scattered around the house. '*Musafir hoon yaroon, naa ghar hai naa thikana, mujhe chalte jaana hai, bas chalte jaana.*'

Besides all the other 'arts' that a lady learns while emerging as a dexterous, multi-talented, proficient army wife, one of the most distinguished skills she masters over years of postings is the art of 'packing' and 'unpacking' almost everything in a house. From the safety pins used to tuck her sari, to the sofas, beds or mattresses, everything gets safely sealed and mindfully unpacked by every prudent military couple who value the hard work that went into earning them.

I had learned a lot of domestic hacks from the more

experienced army wives about how to securely pack stuff and keep them safe for months to come. Even wrapping the glass items with layers of bubble and newspaper was a piece of art and required a lot of patience and diligent thinking. If one whiskey glass breaks, the whole set of twelve is rendered useless. Moreover, due to the dearth of good markets near the military station, preserving the collection is of great importance, as one cannot depend on local shopping most of the time. But before you start feeling remorseful, let me tell you very proudly that such situations do not prevent a military couple from building a plenitude of collectables from each posting.

One morning at 11, my phone rang with my husband's name flashing on it. Getting a call from him during office hours was unusual for me, so I knew in my heart of hearts that '*aa gayi, humari posting aa gayi*'. I picked up the call and immediately asked, '*Kahan aayi hai posting*?'

My husband, in a very low but firm voice, affirmed, '*Haan aa gayi*, start packing.'

With some more details on the place of posting and a brief discussion about the pros and cons of the new station, I put the phone down and took a deep breath, looking around the house. Everything I saw, from the plants in the pots to the pillows on the bed to the curtains on the windows, had to be packed. The scope of work scared me, and I went to grab a glass of water. 'Oh! *Iss fridge ko bhi pack karna hai, iss bottle ko bhi aur iss glass ko bhi*!' At the moment of utter chaos, I could only rely on a cup of garam kadak adrak wali chai for myself, which always lifts my spirits (and now I know why these faujis always keep asking for chai). After my dose of energy booster,

I took the notepad from my husband's desk, also picked a pen and a sketch pen (for some weird reason, I like making my notes with colourful sketch pens!).

Next morning, all the black boxes that had been neatly stacked in our garage were pulled out, dusted, and then painted afresh with another coat of shiny black paint. All of these black beauties were labelled with my husband's name, rank, and serial number for identification purposes.

Meanwhile, while the boxes were drying in the lawn, different tactical plans were being strategized in other corners of the house. In the lawn, under the neem tree, my housemaid was collecting the leaves and putting them to dry for use at the time of packing. The washing machine was whirring with the linens that were ready to be packed. The breakables were being mummified with layers of packaging materials around them. The electrical fittings were being dismantled into pieces and packed in thermocol packaging, which had been preserved from the day it was bought, on the upper shelf of our garage.

In between all this confusion, I was busy with my own chaos. The piles of saris were spread all around my room as if asking me, '*Kuch karo humara.*' I was clueless where to start and where to end. This dilemma was taking up a lot of my time, so I finally settled on the thought that 'at the time of crisis, better to stick to basics'. With those lines on repeat mode in my mind, I packed all the chiffons in one box, all the silks in another, and whatever mix of fabric I was left with in the final box. Smartly enough, I kept one of each kind out in the closet for the 'just in case I need them' moments in the army.

Then came the Herculean task of winding up the kitchen.

The collection of an Indian woman can be broadly summed up in two major areas: her clothes for every occasion and her utensils and spices for any kind of food. I stood clueless in front of the pile of patilas and kadais I had fetched from my mother's kitchen as part of my planning for army life. I was now trying all the permutations and combinations to fit them into the boxes with the rest of the kitchen items. Finally, the art of 'stacking' helped: I placed the smaller patilas in the bigger ones and gradually stacked them all according to size, fitting them tightly in one corner of the biggest box, which was marked as Box No. 22, 'Kitchen Items,' in my list of boxes.

Though initially, I did not believe in listing out the items on the boxes I used to pack, once during an interaction with senior ladies, one mentioned her practice of keeping the packing sorted. She said that she prepared a list of all the items going into a box and numbered them so whenever she needed an item, it's a cinch to track it down. At first, I found this idea very prudent, but when it came time to put it into action, I found it too taxing to note the whole list down. I used to randomly pack my stuff and often ended up being utterly confused during the unpacking process.

So, this time I decided to value the experience and took the advice of the seniors who have mastered the art of packing over years of service in the army. For that, I pulled out a diary, a yearly planner, actually from last year, which had been a gift from the military man in the house, who would apparently be the last person to use such a thing (I wonder why planners are gifted to military men whose nature of work is so volatile!). However, at this moment, it seemed like a great option to convert it into the 'box planner'. With that thought, I started making columns to segregate the boxes and the items in them.

Finally, after filling the pages with extensive detailing of every small item, such as the 'curtain knobs' being packed in box no 25, and the 'sewing kit' packed in box no 30, I, completely exhausted, gave up and left the rest of the items to chance. When I heard the perplexed military man from the other room trying to arrange his files, say, 'Nothing gets lost in the army; look at this diary, it's from my NDA days. Everything will be found, don't worry,' I threw whatever was left into the empty boxes and finally declared, 'Packing ho gayi!'

The empty house seemed so different and often leaves you emotional; it's yet another difficult moment that an army family faces every two years. From the moment one moves into the house to the moment one has to leave is a long journey filled with numerous tough and light moments. One becomes attached to the walls they decorated, the plants they watered, and the roof under which they created memories. It's not easy to stay detached from all this. Loaded with such heavy emotions, that night, when all our belongings were packed systematically (barring a few!) in the boxes, my husband and I stood in the empty room and felt a pang in our hearts. We looked around and then sat on the MES sofas, waiting to hand them over the next morning. The house looked completely emptied, and the pain of attachment tightened our hearts. Soon, I felt the pain shift from my heart to my growling stomach and realized that we had not eaten since the afternoon. I looked at the kitchen and realized that in my exuberance to use my box planner, I had packed everything in the kitchen, and all I was left with was two packets of Maggi. Though we always had the option of going to our neighbour's house or relying on the mess, we opted to have our last supper at the station at home and happily bid goodbye to our place of happiness.

The ongoing electricity issue in the station demonstrated the meticulousness of my packing. As the lights went off, I had to refer to the recently made box planner and take out the candles and emergency light from box no. 13. I felt a sense of pride.

Finally, the last night at our home was spent with a common bowl of Maggi as our dinner in my hand and the emergency light in my husband's. We looked at each other sitting in almost darkness like ghosts and laughed hysterically.

I just said, 'Remember how we used to go to Sartoria in Vasant Vihar and have candlelight dinners?'

He replied, 'Who knew that one day candlelight dinners would be replaced by emergency light dinners!'

I felt a little remorse in his voice, which often gets him down when he sees me compromising with life, leaving my job, leaving my city life. Like all good army husbands, this is one thing military men find difficult to handle. They know deep down that, for them to soar freely in their work, it is always their better halves who hold the ground firmly for them. They are aware of the immense sacrifices a woman in the army makes. The men in uniform can perform their duties without a glitch of worry in their hearts because they know their tough, military-trained wives will always do the needful and hold the fort in their absence.

But for a good military wife like me, it was just another adventurous night to remember. I understood this early in my military life: life is all about perspective, and I consciously tried to keep mine positive, despite the numerous ups and downs that are natural.

Nevertheless, at this moment, I had to cheer him up, as I did not want the last night to be spent in the house sadly. To do that, I knew words would never suffice; therefore, I took the help of music and selected the apt number for the night:

I was standing
All alone against the world outside
You were searching
For a place to hide
Lost and lonely
Now you've given me the will to survive
When we're hungry
Love will keep us alive

And it kept playing on repeat mode. At dawn, when the truck finally arrived, we loaded our memories into it, packed firmly for one more journey to commence and for so many more memories to make…

Epilogue

'*Every real story is a never-ending story.*' – Michael Ende

During a recent summer holiday, I was out of the cantonment walls, back in my previous workplace, New Delhi, a city where I started my career and worked hard to build my identity. It all happened long ago, and today, all that sounds more like the whispers of the past.

I collected my luggage and took a taxi home. Driving through the city, I passed many lanes, turns, and buildings which reminded me of my initial days in this city of opportunities. I was quietly observing them. The thoughts of bygone days of personal accomplishments in this city started throbbing in my heart. I no longer lived here. I took a deep breath and tried putting back my trust in the decisions I made in my life. After all, home is where the heart is! I smiled thinking of my present association with the whole country by the nature of my husband's job rather than identifying myself with just one city.

Finally, I reached my destination. I G-paid the driver and left.

Surprisingly, after an hour, I received a call from my husband, posted in some remote area near the LOC. I was pleasantly surprised to see his name flashing, and picked up the call.

'Hi, have you reached safely?' he asked, keeping his perpetual composure.

'Yes! I have been here for an hour,' I replied with my usual cheerfulness.

'I believe you have forgotten your purse in the taxi you took,' he pointed out.

I turned numb and frantically started searching for it in my bundle of luggage. Then it struck me – how did he know, sitting miles away, that I had left my purse somewhere.

Before I could ask, he said, 'The taxi driver called me. He probably found my number mentioned on the railway ticket which was inside your purse. He is on his way back to you and will reach soon.'

After twenty minutes, the doorbell rang, and I saw the middle-aged taxi driver, soaked in the city's heat and sweat, standing in front of me holding my black purse in his hand.

He smiled and said, 'Madam, your bag.'

And before I could thank him, he added, 'Madam, you were my last passenger. I didn't know whose bag it was, so I opened it and found the railway ticket. I called the number on it. When I saw your card in the bag and realized you are in the army, I thought I should personally return your bag. I also spoke to the sahib. Madam, you people do so much for the country, so I thought if I could be of any help, it would be a great honour for me.'

I thanked the man politely and appreciated the efforts he took to return my bag.

Hours after he had left, I could feel the gleaming pride in his eyes for the army. The purity of deep emotions, the trust, and the respect towards me only because I was a part of this big system called the Indian Army made me reflect on my life.

Is there anything more to be said about my need to write this book?

That night, after hours of deep thinking, I summarized the ten years of my life in one sentence: I gave up city comforts for the confines of the cantonment but that didn't stop me from spreading my wings and evolving in life!

My endeavour through this book is to bring to attention the exceptional quality of life lived in the Indian Army, which is rooted deeply and held strongly by morality, customs, rituals, traditions, and a strong value system we follow and believe in. I also wanted to break the popular cliché that being in the army, being part of an uncompromising system, saps you of energy and makes for a boring austere life.

Various aspects of civilian and military life are deliberated upon in this book, indicating that the solutions in life are always a matter of choice. The book also highlights how military households deal with common yet tough situations. It celebrates the choices an army family makes to overcome all impediments. How an army family embraces the lack of facilities, opportunities, and so-called modern amenities we take for granted in civilian life – the internet, coffee shops, bakery, restaurants, a decent place to shop, banks, mod cons, and roads – and makes a notable impact on society.

The army way of life is unlike anything you can imagine. If I had not been a part of it, I would not have ever known what it entailed. The responsibility of making this 'army way of life' work like a well-oiled machine rests on the shoulders of the real force behind a man, the real force behind the soldiers – the army wives.

Being an army wife myself, I have tried to put forward the story from her perspective. She brings her own charm and personality to the system through her support, compassion, sacrifices, and elegance, which ultimately cements the beliefs of the soldier guarding the borders fiercely that the family left behind is taken care of by the organization he represents.

Given my generally sunny disposition to life, I have endeavoured to keep the flavour of the narrative light, fun, positive, and always topped up with a pinch of humour. I owe my optimism in life to this organization, which has helped me evolve, and enriched and empowered me as a human being.

Acknowledgements

The life of an 'army wife' is often intriguing to the world outside. More often than not it is shrouded in stereotypes created by Indian cinema. I got baptised into the army fifteen years ago, when I got married to a 'fauji' at the age of twenty-seven. At first I felt like a fish out of water. But fifteen years into my marriage, I realize that while being an army wife can be demanding, it offers unparalleled joys and pleasures. Marrying a man in uniform is not just an honour, but entails a life full of drills, thrills and spills. A heartfelt salute to all the remarkable Indian Army wives who wholeheartedly embrace the 'army way of life' and live it fully every single day! These stories of fun and frolic from army life are a tribute to the shared experiences that have moulded me into who I am today. I owe it all to the Indian Army.

I'm deeply grateful to my husband, Saurabh, for sharing his life with me and taking me along in this extraordinary journey. I soar high because I know you are the steady ground I can return to.

Nothing in my life would have been possible without my elder sister Asha, who has been my guiding light and constant hope at every stage. Thank you for always standing by me. This book is a reality because of your unwavering encouragement.

I am what I am today because of my late father. It is he who passed to his six children, the resilient 'Barmola genes'. It is from my ever-smiling mother that people say I have inherited the humour that you may discover in this book. She is the rock-solid pillar of the Barmola clan. A big love to all my siblings. They set lofty goals despite our humble beginnings, and flew high to reach them, inspiring one another.

A big thank you, Sumant Bhaiya, Asha's equal-half, for inspiring at every step in my life; you are an elder brother, a father figure, brother-in-law and so much more, I won't have been here without you guidance and support. You are my beacon of inspiration and unconditional love.

Thank you, the amazing Mamgain family! Your unwavering support is the rocket fuel that propels me into new horizons and chase my dreams!

I want to express my heartfelt gratitude to my editor, Shantanu Ray Chaudhuri, for taking up my book under his wings! In its editorial journey, the book demanded an editor with as much flair for humour as editing proficiency. It found both in him.

Heartfelt thanks to the creative genius Col S. Ramesh, SM, for curating the incredible illustrations; they are bound to make readers smile and appreciate the amazing way in which he captures the essence of the story in his art.

I thank Om Books International for making this book possible!

And finally, to my precious Maira and Karan, my bundles of joy, who fill my life with love and laughter. Writing this book wouldn't have been possible without the happiness you bring me every day!